" Ignite your passion for adventure with Fiona Horne's new book, *Living the Elements*. Drawing from her own personal experiences, Fiona shares intimate wisdom that is both inspiring and transformative as she fearlessly dives into the realms of earth, air, fire, water, and spirit. Through her captivating storytelling and insightful guidance, she takes readers on a thrilling journey where they can discover their own connection to the elements. *Living the Elements* not only empowers witches but also serves as a guide for anyone seeking a deeper understanding of nature's forces and their role within it. Fiona's ability to merge practical knowledge with her personal magical practices makes this book a must-read for individuals looking to awaken their spiritual potential. Whether you are an experienced witch, adventurist, or simply curious about exploring elemental energies, this book offers invaluable insights and tools that go beyond what you find in traditional books on exploring the magic of the elements. Prepare yourself for an exhilarating journey that will leave you inspired, empowered, and energized."

**Michael Herkes,** author of *The GLAM Witch* and *Glamcraft*

" Vivacious, compassionate, courageous, and incredibly sincere, the author weaves marvelous magick to elevate your practice, and bring home the soul change you most desire. Take her hand and dance to the fire of embracing the joyous mystery of life. Fiona—daring, delightful, heart centered compassion—her words can fill your world with the music of positive change if you let them. She is the ultimate glitter witch—because it is her Spirit that gleams brighter than a thousand stars. Don't miss this excellent read."

**Silver Ravenwolf,** author of *Solitary Witch: The Ultimate Book of Shadows for the New Generation* and *Poppet Magick: Patterns, Spells & Formulas for Poppets, Spirit Dolls & Magickal Animals*

# PRAISE FOR THE BOOK

❝ Fiona and I have shared many adventures over many years and in many different countries. Our hearts are wide open to pushing the boundaries of experience in our pursuit of personal and spiritual growth and she has inspired me to journey even more deeply into the wonders of nature—land, sea, and sky. All of my homes have been blessed by Fiona's magical fire dancing.

Living the Elements is a book filled with Fiona's captivating personal stories that invite the reader to awaken to the power and potential that extreme adventure can bring to their lives. With her inspiring guidance, the reader can explore the elements of the natural world in a way that is profoundly magical and intimately empowering."

**Dannii Minogue,** Television Host, Music Artist, Author & Fashion Designer

❝ Fiona Horne is a longtime friend. We share a love of having extreme adventures in different environments—whether we are scuba diving with sharks or jumping out of airplanes around the world. Fiona was there cheering me on when I did my first wingsuit jump with Jeb Corliss at Skydive Perris many years ago.

Fiona continues to impress me with her fearless spirit and her magical life and in her latest book, she guides the reader through adventures that take you from exercises and meditations within the safety of your own home to the very height of an active volcano—and beyond.

Whether you're seeking high adventure or just want to push some of the boundaries of your everyday life, Living the Elements will take you as far as you want to go while helping you discover the magic within yourself and the world around you."

**Roberta Mancino,** World record holding skydiver, BASE jumper, high fashion model, Hollywood stunt woman

" The deeper core of elemental magick! In this approachable, unique, and encouraging book, Fiona expertly guides the reader in active elemental immersion, teaching directly from a plethora of personal experience. Witches, mystics, and spiritual practitioners of all stripes can benefit from Living the Elements. This book has genuinely helped inspire my life; it's amazing how many opportunities await us in this world, no matter who or where we are."

**Raven Digitalis,** author of *The Empath's Oracle* and *A Witch's Shadow Magick Compendium*

" The ultimate guide for the magical adventure seeker! Fiona Horne's Living the Elements focuses on the active witch and the unique magic that accompanies the physical exploration of the earth and its inherent magic. Whether you're a world traveler or a local hiker, this book will feed the soul of every magical wanderer."

**Tonya A. Brown,** Editor in Chief of Witch Way Publishing, Host of The Witch Daily Show and author of *The Door to Witchcraft*

" I'm pretty sure Fiona Horne is the most interesting woman in the world. While I'm almost certain I will never jump out of an airplane and chances are good I will not, in this lifetime, find myself in an underwater restaurant in Dubai, Fiona has inspired me to work with the elements at my own pace, in my own way, in more unique, challenging, and dynamic ways than ever before. While I have long considered elemental magic to be a profound way of shifting my energy and busting out of ruts, until I read this book I honestly didn't even know the half of it. I'm grateful to Fiona for expanding my horizons with her bold examples, frank revelations, and gentle encouragement. If you're interested in elemental magic, you really must read this book."

**Tess Whitehurst,** author of *You Are Magical* and *The Queen Mab Oracle*

# FIONA HORNE
# LIVING
## THE ELEMENTS
### EXTREME ADVENTURES FOR WITCHES

**Warlock Press**™

# LIVING THE ELEMENTS: EXTREME ADVENTURES FOR WITCHES

© 2023, Fiona Horne

All rights reserved. No part of this publication may be reproduced, stored in a retrieval system or transmitted in any form or by any means, electronic, mechanical, photocopying, recording or otherwise without the prior permission of the publisher or in accordance with the provisions of the Copyright, Designs and Patents Act 1988 or under the terms of any license permitting limited copying issued by the Copyright Licensing Agency.

**Published by:**
Warlock Press
1219 Decatur Street
New Orleans, 70116 LA, USA

**Cover Photos by:**
*Earth:* Beki Colada
*Air:* Montana Powell
*Fire:* William Torillo
*Water:* Shawn T. Olson
*Spirit:* Tracy McFie

**Cover Design and Typesetting:** Christian Day
**Interior Photos:** Provided by Fiona Horne
**Copy Editing:** Levi Rowland

ISBN-13: 978-1-7332466-6-8

# CONTENTS

**Prelude** . . . . . . . . . . . . . . . . . . . . . . . . . . . X

## INTRODUCTION TO ADVENTURE     1

The Three Levels of Experience . . . . . . . . . . . . .1
    Transcendent . . . . . . . . . . . . . . . . . . . . . 1
    Potent. . . . . . . . . . . . . . . . . . . . . . . . . . 1
    Passionate . . . . . . . . . . . . . . . . . . . . . . 1
Levels of Extreme . . . . . . . . . . . . . . . . . . . . . .3
Thoughts on Being Extreme . . . . . . . . . . . . . . 6
Some Practical Advice . . . . . . . . . . . . . . . . . . 8
Extreme Adventures Equal Facing Fears . . . . . . . 9
Necessary Fears . . . . . . . . . . . . . . . . . . . . . 10
Elemental Healing . . . . . . . . . . . . . . . . . . . . 15
Sign Up to My Patreon! . . . . . . . . . . . . . . . . 21
Ethical Adventure Travel . . . . . . . . . . . . . . . 22
Balance . . . . . . . . . . . . . . . . . . . . . . . . . . 25
Journaling . . . . . . . . . . . . . . . . . . . . . . . . 25
Spell for Courage . . . . . . . . . . . . . . . . . . . 26

## FIRE     30

Transcendent . . . . . . . . . . . . . . . . . . . . . . 32
    Firedancing . . . . . . . . . . . . . . . . . . . . . . 32
    Climb an Active Volcano . . . . . . . . . . . . . 34
Potent . . . . . . . . . . . . . . . . . . . . . . . . . . 36
    Firewalking . . . . . . . . . . . . . . . . . . . . . . 36
    Explore the Circle of Fire . . . . . . . . . . . . . 37
Passionate . . . . . . . . . . . . . . . . . . . . . . . . 39
    Fire on Film . . . . . . . . . . . . . . . . . . . . . 39
    Campfires and More . . . . . . . . . . . . . . . . 42
Elemental Invocation: Pele . . . . . . . . . . . . . . 42

## WATER — 48

**Transcendent** . . . . . . . . . . . . . . . . . 48
   Scuba Diving . . . . . . . . . . . . . . . . 48
   Freediving . . . . . . . . . . . . . . . . . 56
   Sailing . . . . . . . . . . . . . . . . . . . 60
   Surfing . . . . . . . . . . . . . . . . . . . 65
   Stand Up Paddle Boarding (Sup) . . . . . 69
   Kayaking . . . . . . . . . . . . . . . . . . 72

**Potent** . . . . . . . . . . . . . . . . . . . . . 81
   Waterfalls . . . . . . . . . . . . . . . . . 81

**Passionate** . . . . . . . . . . . . . . . . . . . 84
   Aquariums . . . . . . . . . . . . . . . . . 84
   Underwater Restaurants . . . . . . . . . . 84
   Dive Into Water Movies . . . . . . . . . . 85
   Float Tanks . . . . . . . . . . . . . . . . . 86
   Sunset Sails . . . . . . . . . . . . . . . . 88

**Elemental Invocation: Yemaya** . . . . . . . . 89

## AIR — 93

**Transcendent** . . . . . . . . . . . . . . . . . 93
   Skydiving . . . . . . . . . . . . . . . . . 93
   Flying Airplanes . . . . . . . . . . . . . . 98

**Potent** . . . . . . . . . . . . . . . . . . . . . 103
   Hot Air Ballooning . . . . . . . . . . . . . 103
   Indoor Skydiving . . . . . . . . . . . . . 105
   Zipline Magic . . . . . . . . . . . . . . . 110
   Paraglide in Turkey . . . . . . . . . . . . 111

**Passionate** . . . . . . . . . . . . . . . . . . . 111
   Glass Bottom Bridges . . . . . . . . . . . 111
   Walking Over a Suspension Bridge . . . . 112
   Kite Flying . . . . . . . . . . . . . . . . . 113
   Movies About Flight . . . . . . . . . . . . 115

**Elemental Invocation: Isis** . . . . . . . . . . 116

# EARTH — 120

## Transcendent — 120
- Meditation Within the King's Chamber — 120
- Survivor — 123
- Hike the World's Most Dangerous Hiking Trail — 125

## Potent — 128
- Dunes — 128
- The Crystal Mountain in the Western Desert — 130
- Road Trip to Vegas — 130
- Wilderness Immersion — 131
- Bucket List: Underground at Göbekli Tepe — 133

## Passionate — 134
- Read — 134
- Caves Road Southwest Australia — 134
- Tv Binge on Survival Reality Shows — 137
- Gardening — 139

## Elemental Invocation: Gaia — 140

# SPIRIT — 142

## Transcendent — 142
- Dark Retreats — 142
- Vipassana — 146

## Potent — 151
- Yoga — 151
- Temazcal Retreats — 153

## Passionate — 157
- Meditation — 157
- Astronomy — 157

## Sobriety — 166

## Personal Evolution — 166

## Elemental Invocation: Self — 168

## About the Author — 174

# PRELUDE

Get ready to experience the sacred elements of Witchcraft in an action-packed dynamic way that enlivens every fiber of your being and supercharges your spell casting. Air, Earth, Fire, Water, and Spirit are at the core of our magickal work and in this book, I will give you inspiring ideas on how to interact with these elements, invoking your most empowered self on the path of the best Witch you can be.

### THERE ARE THREE LEVELS TO EXPLORE:

*Transcendent*—nothing between you and pure exhilaration!

*Potent*—intensely liberating!

*Passionate*—the seed is planted!

With my help you can decide which one you fit…or maybe work through all three levels!

A long time ago, after releasing my first book, I received a wonderful handwritten letter posted from India (this was before emails and smart phones). A girl who had read my first book said because of me she had decided to face her fears and do some extraordinary things—she learned to scuba dive in Thailand, and she was about to hike to base camp at Mt. Everest. It was humbling and thrilling to receive this message and know that I had made this impact on her life. Once, I received an email from a 73-year young lady who read my autobiography, *The Naked Witch*, and said that I had made her realize she still had a few adventures in her yet!

And so, I hope you share your adventures with me! It's easy—contact me through my socials and let's inspire each other!

**Instagram:** @captainfifi    **Facebook:** @fionahorneofficial

### A SCAVENGER RELIGION

My dear friends and publishers, Brian Cain and Christian Day, once called Witchcraft a "scavenger religion" (a quote that comes from Maxine Sanders) for how we align with various deities, traditions, and practices from different civilizations and cultures. I love that they said this, and I think it is because we are misunderstood and have had to address so many misconceptions about our spiritual paths that we seek to venerate the panoply of humanity's divine presence and recognition. It's not a lack of respect—it is a celebration. When I was in Egypt recently during the writing of this book, I received very intense messages that we are not to ask anything of the Goddesses and Gods, only venerate them and let them decide what is best for us.

And so, the rituals in this book are offered in the spirit of worship and respect. The Gods will be pleased, and their light shall shine on us.

## WHAT TO DO

How does this book work? There is a chapter for each element and in each chapter, activities aligned with each element are offered. Each element has three levels. **PASSIONATE, POTENT**, and **TRANSCENDENT**.

## FIRST

Consider which element you want to work on and invoke more powerfully into your life. For example, I have had a lot of Spirit, Air, Fire, and Water energies invoked in my life. As I wrote this book, I realized I wanted to work with Earth more and embrace that sense of being anchored and grounded in an empowered way to facilitate tapping into physical manifestation and source—to heal pains and aches and exhaustion in this physical form and find more comfort in my nomadic life.

## SECOND

Choose your activity and your level.

The three levels consider different physical conditions, even financial—but it's important to face this book with excitement and a spirit of adventure. That's why you bought it, right?

Work your way through the three levels, in either direction, to fully explore all aspects of living with your chosen element.

## THIRD

Honor the elemental deity with the ritual suggested in each section.

## FOURTH

Cast your spell for courage, featured on page 26, and go forth and do it!

## FIFTH

Share what you learned—you can't have something unless you can give it away. Tell people how empowering it is to stretch your boundaries and do things you never thought possible! Encourage them to explore supercharging their lives with extreme adventures too!

> "We grow through discomfort and insight…never through apathy."
>
> Vishen Lakhiani (*The Buddha and the Badass*—Rodale Publishing)

Sunrise with the Sphinx, Giza, Egypt

## JOIN ME IN AN ADVENTURE!

Do you want to have an incredible life adventure with me? From 2024, I will be conducting adventure retreats and journeys around the world at amazing places that have connected with my heart.

Visit *fionahorne.com* and subscribe to my mailing list to be the first to know about opportunities to travel with me and change the way you live!

**Website:** www.FionaHorne.com

# INTRODUCTION TO ADVENTURE

This book shares my love of extreme adventures and the stories of some of the ones that have immersed me in elemental wisdom and communion in ways I never anticipated. Most of the adventures in this book are things I have done, and some are things I am dreaming of doing. Creating this book is inspiring me as much as I hope it is inspiring you! There are so many brilliant, amazing, blessed things to enjoy and learn from on this extraordinary planet. And some of humanity's best creative efforts allow us to dive in deeply and experience the sacred elemental natural world in truly profound ways.

## THE THREE LEVELS OF EXPERIENCE

### TRANSCENDENT
The extreme experience on the razor edge of the most radical adventure!

### POTENT
The extraordinary experience that is all-consuming and yet in the middle of the path!

### PASSIONATE
The armchair experience where your mind takes you there!

## WHAT TO EXPECT

This book is not the ultimate guide to every extreme adventure on the planet—there are books like *1001 Things to Do Before You Die*…this is not that book! But it *is* full of amazing activities that you can try to make your life profoundly full of magickal adventure! I hope that by sharing some of my experiences and stories that you will feel inspired and confident to create your own experiences and tell your own stories to others. Plugging back into your extreme elemental energy by reliving your experiences when sharing and inspiring others is powerful magick.

By no means is this an exhaustive list but I hope it will inspire you and motivate you to explore extraordinary opportunities and adventures in a magickal way to supercharge your powers. Plug into the wellspring of universal experience and wisdom that is inherent in every deep and sincere interaction with the elements. These five building blocks of our natural magickal world: Earth, Air, Fire, Water, and Spirit, just like the five musical notes, create an infinite magickal melody that can empower, inspire, and delight your senses, your mind, your heart, and your soul. These magickal extreme adventures can clean up your life from residual past life fear and baggage, clearing your energetic layers in this life to be elevated in the next, and even more importantly than that, elevated in your life NOW.

I have also tried to offer as many options for as many budgets as possible. Like we do in spellcasting, we swap out ingredients where we need to—we trust our gut and get creative. So, you may read about rafting under the Iguazú Falls of Chile…but you are in

Wisconsin. Well, is there an option near you that offers a similar experience? Yes! Big Manitou Falls. And while you cannot raft under those falls, you can get close enough that you can feel the spray on your face! So don't be afraid to substitute and get extreme in your backyard. Though, sometimes the commitment it takes to create an extraordinary experience of travel, or saving money, or getting a job that plants you in the midst of your extreme adventure is part of the Transcendent process!

> **Adventure Witch Tip!**
> Start with Passionate and work your way up to Transcendent! #goals

Which brings me to another immersion point: research the natural origins of the area you are blending with—geological and geographical. Learn the origins, explore, and consider all the ingredients of this experience with your human brain…get to know your immersion environment as much as it is going to get to know you. It will deepen your experience on every level—not only the elemental one you are aligning with.

## LEVELS OF EXTREME

You can jump out of an airplane…but is that plane over Mt. Everest, or over ancient Egyptian pyramids?! I have jumped out of airplanes in many places around the world. But recently on my first trip to Egypt, I was staying next to the pyramids of Giza and one day I heard an airplane and looked up and saw parachutes open and come down over the pyramids. When I saw those tandem masters landing in the surrounding busy Cairo suburb, dodging cars, donkeys, and pedestrians in the hot gusty desert conditions, I thought, "OMG that is so dangerous and radical!" But of course, the skydive tandem masters were experts, and everyone landed safely and cheering in joy. Does this mean that jumping out over the pyramids is more extreme than jumping at your local drop zone?

No! Or yes, if you want it to!

Firedancing
(Photo by Marjo Aho)

> **LIVE THE ADVENTUROUS LIFE OF YOUR DREAMS**
>
> Take an energized step today, no matter how small, towards living with Adventure.
>
> Do one thing you have never done before (this can just mean taking a different route to work!).
>
> Express yourself in a new way (as simple as wearing a color or an item of clothing you never have before).
>
> Connect with new people (strike up a conversation with someone you have not met before).
>
> Or reconnect with a loved one in a fresh new way (surprise them with something you've never offered them before—this might mean a gift, or a smile, or a compliment…anything that will create a spirit of adventure between you).

In this book I am not going to advocate the extreme of the extreme experiences—I'm going to use my own experiences as a measure. I mean, if I can do it—you can!

Obviously, my friend, professional skydiver and Hollywood stuntwoman, Roberta Mancino, who does stunts for the Avengers and Mission Impossible movies and regularly jumps off a 4000-foot rock face in Norway wearing high heels for fashion magazine photoshoots, is going to have more extreme experiences than me jumping out of a hot air balloon at 2,500 feet in California.

But I loved that jump! It put a smile on my face for days!

And that's the point—don't compare your extreme experiences to another. Use my guide to get out of your comfort zone and immerse yourself in your chosen element. And tap into your unique and awesomely valuable experience.

> **TAKE TIME TO TAP IN**
>
> Have an authentic adventure.
>
> Don't compare your experience to another.
>
> Don't rush—even during an adrenaline event you should have time to breathe and relax and soak it all up.
>
> Take time to tap in, be present, and embody your element.

# THOUGHTS ON BEING EXTREME

Is walking an extreme activity?

Once I was in an abusive relationship and the daily attacks ultimately manifested in extreme pain in my hip—both a physical injury and emotional too, as all my grief and anger got stored there. Spiritually, pain in the hips represents trauma and shame. I walked with a limp for nearly two years as I tried to get on with my life on the outside. When I physically left the relationship, my hip started to heal, which I helped along with adjustments from a trusted osteopathic healer. I also started the inner work to heal the emotional trauma that was being held in my hip. It took a few months, but eventually walking longer distances, without too much pain, became possible. I didn't have to adjust my plans based on how much pain I would experience and how my hip would lock up and slow me and anyone else I was with down. I could just get up and go for a walk…

maybe not a jog or a run, but definitely a walk.

The day I realized I was pain free and able to walk without limping was extraordinary. Until then I had been doing the inner work to make peace with this "perceived" permanent condition, to understand that I would need to be able to find joy in life despite experiencing movement in this limited way. It was a metaphor for the life I lived with him, trapped and controlled and in ever growing fear of him. He had trained me to think that this was the way the rest of my life would be, and I should accept it and find a new version of "happiness" as he determined it should be. But on this day, I had done a beautiful deep freedive, extending my personal best depth. While held in the loving embrace of the Great Mother Ocean, I realized I could let go of my fear of him. And I felt this tremendous sense of rebirth and gratitude and trust in the processes of life—that it really wants us to feel and be the joy that is at the core of all Creation. And sometimes surviving extreme suffering is the most potent way to feel this.

And to just know that the magick we conjure works—on all levels in every way if we allow it to.

How did I leave? It was a strategic mission…it was an extraction… there were many events. There was help offered from female friends and experts in getting out of abusive situations, but I had to accept it. And as bad and worse as the abuse was getting daily, I was convinced that I couldn't leave him. If I just changed myself a little more, if I was just careful not to do the things that upset him, then it would all be ok and we could be in love and together. But then there was the day I did this spell…with feathers I had gathered from around where I lived with him, with rocks gathered from sacred places aligned with the area I was in. I removed everything from my altar…and conjured a new reality—one that allowed me to let go of the "love" I so desperately wanted to "work," which had become something very toxic and bad.

I anchored in my life the clearing of the path which revealed to me the way out. It took three more months and I had to give up everything, my band, my car, my home…and the dream of what I had hoped so much we would be.

But the spell helped me plant seeds for new dreams, and I walked through Egypt's ancient temples and pyramids in the wake of the loss of us…and my life's adventures continue.

And so, walking is extreme to me…extremely brilliant, extremely beautiful, extremely freeing, extremely appreciated…an affirmation that no matter what, life can change for the better, peace can come, and adventures are always there to be had.

## SOME PRACTICAL ADVICE

Maybe it's the commercial pilot in me, but I weigh up risk versus reward when it comes to extreme adventures. As I write this, I am on the eve of travelling to Dubai where my friend works as a pilot for Skydive Dubai, and I love jumping there and dodging camels in the desert as I land. Then I am on to Egypt to walk a lot, exploring the pyramids and temples. So, I have decided not to skydive at the start of my trip…if I do jump it will be after Egypt, in the four days I head back to Dubai…just in case I have a hard landing.

Once upon a time I would have just thought, "Fuck it- don't be a wuss, just jump!" But now I have learned I experience more freedom, mental and physical, by being authentically motivated and trusting in the adventures of the Universe I take…and letting myself say "no" or "not now," sometimes!

But I really want to embody the transformative element of Air and let it work its magick in my life, so I am going to jump and fly on Xline, the world's longest urban zipline that runs through the middle of Dubai as soon as I get there!

# EXTREME ADVENTURES EQUAL FACING FEARS

Otherwise, what is the point? I have always found that the best adventures are the ones I'm scared of! Whether its sitting in the lotus position for 14 hours at a Vipassana retreat or jumping out of an airplane…with 12 others attempting a world record! (The idea of jumping out of an airplane alone never scared me!)

Facing fear can be the foundation for a profound spiritual awakening. But that doesn't mean that every extreme adventure embodying the five sacred elements must be scary. But hopefully each one on every level is confronting in some way, to shake up your edges and extend your boundaries and parameters of what you CAN do.

Use the suggestions in this book to get out of your comfort zone. For example, after a steady diet of TikTok videos and Instagram scrolling, it might be terrifying to you to commit to and prioritize reading a book! Use this aversion to fuel your intention. Make reading a book an extreme adventure in itself!

*Find out how you could be facing fear to create the foundation for true spiritual awakening.*

Do I get scared? Yes! Most recently at a deep dive at Elphinstone Reef in the Red Sea of southern Egypt. I was recovering from a cold and I did not feel 100%; my chest was tight, but I could equalize. The water was rough—there was a big swell that day and it was a grueling ride out in the zodiac (an inflated speed boat). Because I was tired and recovering, the sense of excitement I had to be finally diving after being in bed on my holiday for two days was replaced with a sense of panic and fear as I descended. How did I keep my shit together? That will be explained in a few pages!

The point is that having extreme adventures means you are going to find out how extremely collected and capable you can be! And often that shift of psychic awareness creates a profound spiritual awakening as the perception of the physical boundary of "self" lifts and you experience a transcendental sense of bliss. And the ongoing experience becomes even more profound.

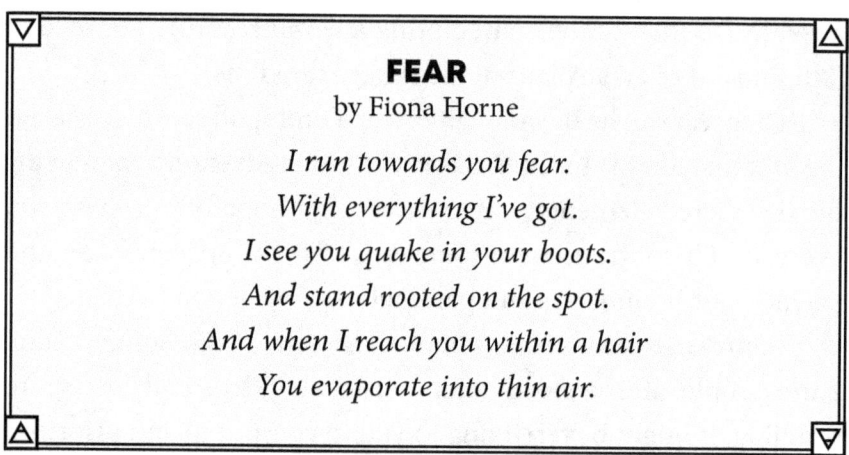

**FEAR**
by Fiona Horne

*I run towards you fear.*
*With everything I've got.*
*I see you quake in your boots.*
*And stand rooted on the spot.*
*And when I reach you within a hair*
*You evaporate into thin air.*

## NECESSARY FEARS

Yes, I'm still talking about fear! Because we must unlock our relationship with fear in order to transmute, in an alchemical way, the elemental energies we wish to invoke and embody…and be transformed by.

Fear itself is natural and a necessary part of being alive. It's genetically programmed into us to keep us alive and free from "harm."

Fear signals us not to step off a cliff, to hit the brakes if the car in front of us stops suddenly, or to quickly duck and cover if we hear gunfire (sad I must include that example as a common event these days). The problem is when fear works overtime because we are stressed, tired, over-stimulated, or even bored.

> *I have been through some terrible things in my life, some of which actually happened."*
> —Mark Twain

The Sossusvlei Sand Dunes of Namibia

As much as I've made the effort to be enlightened and empowered when it comes to feeling liberated from fear, I have spent a lot of time fearful and worried. About vague things. Funnily enough, when I stand in the doorway of a plane, ready to jump out, I just feel happy and excited. It's when I wake up at 3 a.m. with my head full of dark non-specific thoughts, that something is wrong with me, my life, my choices, and I am feeling irrationally riddled with imposter syndrome and deep sadness, that I am afraid.

> **ONE MINUTE MEDITATION**
>
> My new favorite one minute meditation came to me in a dream (yes, one of those moments I woke up at 3 a.m.). But instead of feeling panicked I felt good, with a clear memory of the dream which I now harness as a visualization and use regularly.
>
> I am driving fast along a desert highway in a vintage sports car—top down, Thelma and Louise style. There are giant billboards lining the road and the names of my fears are emblazoned on them.
>
> And I am just roaring by and leaving them in the dust!
>
> And if you haven't heard of *Thelma and Louise*, search this movie online and watch it! The original female road warrior movie of freedom from fear in the face of social oppression—the ending always makes me cry tears of admiration and joy.

Eventually, I manage to go back to sleep by getting out of bed, writing some things I am grateful for in my journal, and then putting on a relaxing audio sleep story with my favorite App called "Calm."

More often than not, I wake up feeling fine.

Right now, I'm filled with fear that I will never finish this book! LOL! It takes disciplined thought to address that fear, and just keep tapping away at my keyboard.

How many times has what we feared not happened and everything has been fine? All those moments we spent obsessively being fearful could have been filled with love, trust, confidence, optimism, and excitement, but instead were smothered with fear that was more habitual than rational.

*Mindful* is now a popular catch word in mainstream culture. The Cambridge Dictionary defines the word as: "Deliberately aware of your body, mind and feelings in the present moment in order to create a feeling of calm."

"Full of mind" is my definition, and often my mind is the problem! So, I would like to offer a Witch's interpretation of being in the present moment and allowing a sense of calm empowerment to suffuse us.

Separate from the "mind"—like we do in spellcasting or when casting Circle and open up to that space of infinite potential and creation. To consciously "expand into" this space, take a deep breath and send your awareness to the palms of your hands and the soles of your feet. When I do this, they always begin to tingle.

From here, scan your body—notice where there is tightness and tension. Consider the stories your mind is telling you. Listen from your soul's perspective. Pull your awareness far out enough to get a glimpse or even a firm view of the grand picture of existence—you are one with everything; there are reasons for everything; there are answers for everything.

Don't take yourself so seriously. Don't think what you have to share, what you desire to experience, is NOT important. It is! You are here—and that is meant to be. Soften your tightness, soften your frustration, soften your fear. And enjoy doing this in an extreme way!

Be kind to yourself when you are filled with doubt, or even apathy. Sometimes you will think, "What's the point?" "This is dumb." "I've changed my mind and I don't want to do it anymore."

Face these moments of self-doubt with courage and compassion. Just tell yourself the opposite:

"I am the point."

"This is awesome."

"I'm excited about my decision to do this."

"Let's go!"

> **TWO VISUALIZATIONS TO HELP ANXIETY**
> These two visualizations can be done many times throughout the day to help with nervous tension or anxiety, especially if you are starting to really take conscious steps out of your comfort zone and explore activities and approaches to life offered in this little book!
>
> 1. Imagine your thoughts like clouds in the sky, drifting past and away into the blue.
>
> 2. Visualize a flowing stream, with each thought a leaf, twirling slowly away downstream.

All the world's "problems" are craftily guilt tripped onto us by corporations that would like us to be paralyzed into a passive state of consumer-based fear. Basically, we just buy their products, take their ineffective medicines, and pay our "carbon taxes", while they merrily private jet around the world, buying multimillion-dollar AI-designed homes with "purified air and water" (because their companies have polluted the waterways and cut down the forests). That 1% *elite* in their private jets and giant personal car collections contribute to more pollution and carbon emissions than the entirety of humanity. This disparity can often have me feeling depressed and exhausted with the human condition.

Most recently I found myself repeating like a mantra:

"Don't take yourself so bloody seriously Fiona. Enjoy your life. You have a right to be here."

And I go and have an extreme adventure to affirm this fact!

# ELEMENTAL HEALING
## Extreme Adventures Can Heal Grief, Despair, and Trauma

In recent years, I have felt so much grief that it's paralyzing. I was in Egypt for the first time having an extraordinary experience—in two ways. One, because Egypt is extraordinary, and two because I was on a tour that had promised to be an intimate spiritual experience. It was anything but. It was more like being part of a reality show with 20 other participants, a large proportion of whom carried on like it was a frat party. So disappointing and exhausting…and yet, I was there…I had to make the best of it I could.

Luckily, Egypt resonated so powerfully with me on a deep spiritual and genetic level that I did have profound, revelatory experiences, despite the trip not being what I was told it would be when I bought my ticket.

Finally, my time with the group ended and I left on my own to have a meditative diving experience in the South Red Sea. I was feeling a bit better, and healing from the trauma of Bon Jovi's "Living on a Prayer" playing as we were in the tour bus heading to Dendera Temple Complex (sacred to Hathor, the Goddess of music and love, who surely would have suggested something else to play on our way to venerate her). Then I received a text and was told that my beloved island dog, Fifi, whom I was to be with in just two weeks, had been put to sleep without any consultation with me. The grief and despair and shock were sickening and bewildering (they still are…I will never get over this happening to my baby), but I must make peace with it.

Freediving with Dolphins at Sataya Reef, South Red Sea

What has this got to do with living an adventurous life? Exploring extreme adventures doesn't mean you are running away from difficult experiences or traumatic events—instead they can equip you with a sense of resilience and courage to deal with life's everyday challenges.

## MY 5-STEP GUIDE TO CALM A PANIC ATTACK

Believe it or not, I have had panic attacks—a memorable one being when scuba diving on a wreck off the coast of Espiritu Santo Island in Vanuatu. I descended into the wreck of the *SS Coolidge*, sunk by underwater mines during WW2. My goal was to witness "The Lady", an infamous porcelain sculpture of a woman riding a white unicorn…originally an adornment of one of the ship's smoking rooms when it was a luxury passenger liner.

As I approached her, I felt excited…but then incredibly claustrophobic. My hair stood on end, and I felt nauseous, and my heart started to pound really hard. I wanted to bolt to the surface, but it wasn't an option—I was at 39 meters (127 feet)—a fast ascent would mean a strong likelihood of the bends (a potentially deadly condition of nitrogen bubbles building up in your blood stream and getting lodged in your joints and soft tissues…think strokes and paralysis and other fun stuff!). Why did I have a sudden onset panic attack? I was tired that day—I had a big night the night before at a kava ceremony in the village, and I was on malaria medication which made me feel a bit off-color (I've never taken it since—horrible stuff). So, when my mind slipped into panic and my body followed suit, I had to get a grip. The following steps are essentially what I did.

### STEP 1: MAKE PANIC YOUR FRIEND

When you feel that surge of panic, greet it like you would a friend. Say hello to it. Acknowledge it. Don't let it run around like crazy inside you. In my case, underwater, I stepped back from the feeling enough for a moment to acknowledge it. I remember saying in mind, "Oh hello, aren't you interesting?"

The feeling became something separate for long enough that I did not feel overtaken by it. Doing this helps your spiraling thoughts calm down…like the rest of these steps do.

### STEP 2. FOCUS ON WHERE YOU PHYSICALLY ARE

This helps you be focused in the moment. It made sense to me at the time to look at the shipwreck. I thought, "I am in front of a metal doorway. There is an orange fish swimming over a small lump of hard coral." I found myself talking into my regulator so I could hear my voice. Talking to yourself is a really good idea when panic starts to rise up. It anchors you in the tangible, calming physical world—not the imaginary scary one. I found myself saying, "I am feeling calm and relaxed. I don't want to be 'that' person. I am ok." "That" person meaning the one that panicked and bolted from the dive, that all the other divers will gossip about. (Sometimes ego is a good thing haha!)

### STEP 3: BREATHE SLOWLY AND EXPANSIVELY

As this panic attack came on, my breathing became very rapid—not great when you are on scuba—you don't want to suck up all your air fast. So, I made a conscious effort to slow my exhalations. I was breathing out for twice as long as I was breathing in. You are not supposed to hold your breath on scuba, as trapping air inside your lungs can cause lung expansion injury if you ascend even just a few meters (10-15 feet). You have to always keep your airways open when breathing compressed air. So, I breathed in and then breathed out really slowly. I focused on the sound of the bubbles as I exhaled. Focusing on your breath really helps you anchor and ground and triggers your "panic friend" to settle down very quickly.

## STEP 4: HUG YOURSELF

Yes, giving yourself a hug helps. Be kind to yourself—you've got this, and you've got you. Put your arms around your waist or across your chest with your hands on your shoulders and squeeze a little. Just relax and love yourself for a moment. My version of a hug underwater that time was putting a comforting hand on my regulator as I looked at my air gauge. I had plenty of air in my tank and my regulator was snug in my mouth. I was breathing and everything was ok.

## STEP 5: SMILE

I've said in recent years that I know the secret of an instant face lift—it's called a smile! Smiling doesn't just look appealing, it feels appealing. And if you can make your body smile (even if you must fake it at first), it's amazing how your mind will follow. Underwater I had a regulator in my mouth, but as I calmed down, I found myself smiling. And it was at this time my dive buddy who had entered the wreck ahead of me swam back and gave me a questioning ok signal as they could see I had paused before penetrating the wreck. The four steps above happened quite quickly. I was able to nod back to my buddy and give an ok signal back and continue the dive. I kept smiling all the way to "The Lady".

So, if you are faking your smile on land, make sure you keep smiling for at least two to three minutes to really transform all residue of panic and be in the moment to relax, have fun, and then give yourself another hug for being awesome and keeping your shit together.

When I am out of my comfort zone and something bad happens,

I actually find I am ready with more resources to handle the confronting mental, emotional, and physical challenges.

Maybe you will too. Padding your life with a cotton wool or a bubble wrap approach and not putting yourself out there does not protect you—it limits you finding out what you are capable of.

I offer that while there is a lot of adventure in this book—there is not every adventure in the known Universe! So, consider getting a book like: *The Bucket List: Nature, Incredible Adventures in the Natural World*, by Kath Stathers (Murdoch Books, 2018). The book's pitch says it best:

> *The Bucket List: Nature takes readers on a global journey of the world's most amazing wildlife, visiting forests, deserts, savannahs, mountains, and oceans. From action-packed adventures (camel trekking in Jordan, diving in the Maldives), to relaxing experiences (savoring the peace of a Giant Redwood Forest), to conservation-themed vacations including working as a Giant Panda keeper in China, caring for wounded elephants in Thailand, and guarding baby turtles as they make their way to the ocean in Costa Rica. This book has it all. The Bucket List: Nature is the ultimate wishlist for the dedicated globetrotter or armchair traveler alike. Illustrated with stunning photography, the text provides all the information and practical advice you need to appreciate animals and plants in their natural habitats.*

And use your witchy insight and energy gained from reading this book to enchant any elemental adventure in your life! I look forward to hearing about YOUR adventures!

Feeding Vitamins to a Rescued Bengal Tiger at Big Paw Sanctuary Dubai

# SIGN UP TO MY PATREON!

Let's get to know each other's magick! For my Patreon community I offer my Self Care Sunday show that I bring you from wherever I am in the world. Places like a big cat rescue sanctuary in Dubai, the shore of the Red Sea in Egypt, Hexfest in New Orleans, and the Côte d'Azur of the French Riveria. I often have interesting special guests who offer their motivational insights and personal self-care rituals.

My goal is to inspire and empower you to have a magickal and adventuresome week.

There's lots more on offer for my Patreon family including monthly spells, audio/video versions of my books, and opportunities to chat one on one.

**Website:** www.Patreon.com/fionahorne

# ETHICAL ADVENTURE TRAVEL

Many of the adventures I share and offer here have occurred, or could occur, in parts of the world that are sensitive to exploitation, environmental damage, cultural appropriation, and more.

How do we ensure that our extreme adventures are ethical, considering we are seeking to do magickal work aligning with elemental energy? How can we do our best to make sure our efforts are energetically elevated on every level?

Here is an example when I went to Egypt as part of a group tour. We were given an activity to ride ATVs and camels around the pyramids in Giza. At first, I did not want to partake in this activity. When I looked at the pyramids, I was awestruck in reverence of them. To carry on riding around them in the sand dunes on a variety of transportation methods seemed exploitative. But because I am a bit of a people-pleaser, I went along with the group and did it even though my toes were curling up in my sandals as we roared along on the noisy ATVs with many other humans around me doing the same thing…and the magnificent silent pyramids looming over us. We eventually pulled up at the top of a dune and got on camels and rode them across the sand. There were other people doing the same thing everywhere. Tourists and locals were riding horses across the dunes at great speed…everyone seemed to be having a marvelous time.

I saw something on the sand in front of us. It was large, and as I approached it, I realized to my horror that it was a dead horse. Recently deceased, it smelled strongly, and its teeth were pulled back over its gums, a sad sight of an animal that had died in duress.

Holding a Baby Nile River Crocodile, Aswan, Egypt

Our tour guide walked past the animal smiling, completely unmoved. It was then I noticed a number of other horses lying dead in the sand, and some camels too. Some just skeletons and some still with thin, parched skin remaining over their bones.

In a situation like this it's not appropriate to judge, and it's not possible to stop. The only decision I could make was to never support a tourism activity like this again.

When the opportunity arose (after this group tour) for me to create my own bespoke experiences of Egypt, partnering with a local travel agency, the first thing I told them was that I did not want my guests doing this activity. There are ethical camel rides that happen in places where the camels are loved and supported. There are opportunities to spend time with Arabian horses where they are loved and nurtured and not ridden to death.

These are the places I will take my groups to and support financially.

So, when attempting to be an ethical adventure seeker, do your best to research the company and operators you are giving your money to, and favor those that do their best to ensure ethical and responsible activities and minimally negative impacts.

Respect the cultural differences of places you travel. If it's appropriate, cover your skin. There's no need to make a big statement. When I travel in the Middle East, I like covering up. There's one really practical aspect to wearing a hijab or a burka: they protect you from the searing rays of the sun! Which I'm quite sure is why they were invented in the first place, and then were just appropriated by the patriarchy when it gained a disproportionate control of human activity.

The biggest takeaway I hope to offer is: be respectful, be conscious, and still be you and have the experience that is aligned with your elemental empowering goals. By working with your environment and not against it you are more likely to have a truly empowering and life-changing experience.

## BALANCE

Notice what activities you are drawn towards.

Are you diving into all the Water activities and neglecting the others?

Sometimes what you are drawn towards rationally or emotionally is the opposite of what would best benefit and balance you.

Try to balance your elemental experiences with each other.

You can work magick with blended elemental exchange and invocation.

Water and Earth.

Air and Fire.

And consider always anchoring with a Spirit activity.

Spirit will bless and inspire all of your activities because it gives wings to the moment of ascension beyond the physical place. Where you are not bound by form and instead given an opportunity to observe it in this timeline and space. This opportunity is the seed that grows all these extreme adventures.

## JOURNALING

Keep a journal of your extreme adventures. I have kept journals since I was seven years old. I encourage you to keep a record of all your adventures, of how you felt before you did them and how you felt after.

As Witches we tend to keep track of our magickal activities by recording them traditionally by hand in our book of shadows, or online, or just on our laptops in a word doc.

The wonderful thing about recording your adventures is that you can relive them on days you're feeling low or coming down from the adrenaline of the experience itself.

It's normal to have an energy dip after achieving something extraordinary, and your Extreme Elemental Adventures journal will really help you navigate those days when you are forgetting how awesome you are.

# SPELL FOR COURAGE

*Courage is the confidence to believe in myself.*

As you embark upon elevating your life with extreme adventures, I encourage you to perform this spell—it is a great one because you can literally recharge its intentions and energies by ringing the bell after it is initially cast.

**You will need:**

Brass bell

Orange candle

Carnelian

Courage incense (see recipe below)

Carnelian is aligned with sun energy and helps release self-doubt, empowering you to take assertive action. This is an energizing crystal that can help overcome laziness and its powerful vibration raises self-confidence and stokes the fires of courage in your belly, helping you move past fear, stretch your boundaries, and get out of your comfort zone.

We are born with courage and confidence—they are essential energies for life, but they can get left by the wayside in our busy, overstimulated lives. Confidence can affect a lot of things. It can help us face our fears, make decisions that are in line with our heart, and it can help us honor our truth and show up from a place of stability and purpose.

This spell uses the fourth letter of the Greek alphabet, Delta, represented as the isosceles triangle which is the strongest of all shapes. In mathematics, it represents change, and as numbers are a universal force, we will invoke the energy of change in this spell to transform self-doubt or apathy into dynamic courage.

As you cast this spell for courage, visualize the 3 equal-angled and equal-sided isosceles triangle as a portal for you to step through into your life as an awakened, enlightened, bold, and brave being. Change can make us stronger, more resilient, and whole. So, invoke the essence of courage through the visualization of a gold delta triangle—and with courage and confidence invoked we can handle anything.

### Make your own incense for courage as follows:

Tip: Freeze your mortar and pestle bowl and the frankincense for 30 minutes before grinding and blending. This makes it easier to grind (as it is a gum it can get sticky).

3 teaspoons of frankincense gum

1 teaspoon of ethically sourced dragon's blood powder* (if you need to grind it, I suggest putting it in the freezer for 30 mins too)

3 drops of rose, geranium, OR pine needle oil

A pinch of black pepper

*Note: Dragon's blood powder is sourced from the resin of the *Dracaena draco* tree which is endangered in its natural environment due to over farming. There is another source of dragon's blood powder now being sustainably offered from the fruit of the Javanese *Daemonorops draco* tree. The scales of the fruit secrete a resin that offers similar magickal and medicinal qualities. Be sure when you purchase dragon's blood resin or powder that you are buying ethically sourced magickal ingredients and educate yourself as to where they come from.

Grind the resins separately then mix together in a bowl, add the oil one drop at a time mixing further and then add the pinch of ground black pepper.

Note: it is better to make this courage incense in small batches. This will be enough for 3 weeks at one spell casting a week.

Burn your courage incense on a charcoal disc in a firesafe dish.

Note: it is vastly more empowered to make your own incense, but if this is not an option, use one stick each of frankincense, dragon's blood, and pine, rose, or geranium—three total.

Carve your initials or magickal name in the orange candle, lick your thumb, and trace over the carving with your spit, making it yours.

Light the incense.

Douse yourself with the smoke (using your hands, splash your face and body with the smoke).

Hold the carnelian to the candle so that the flame shines on the crystal and lights it up.

Close your eyes and visualize the golden isosceles Delta of change in front of you and say this invocation of courage out aloud or in your head.

*In my light no shadows be*
*Courage fills me with creativity*
*In my light no shadows be*
*Courage for eternity*
*For the good of all but mostly for me*

Open your eyes and move the bell through the incense smoke, ringing it as you do.

Anytime you need to charge up the spell during the week, ring the bell.

Snuff the flame and the spell is complete.

Carry the carnelian with you in an orange pouch or in your

pocket as a courage charm whilst you plan and undertake your extreme adventures.

**Ocean Life in the Islands**
(Photo by Dave MacVean)

# FIRE

The element of Fire is so fascinating. Growing up I remember I loved nothing more than lighting a fire out in the dark Australian bush and staring into the flames for hours, feeding twigs into its belly to keep it going as long as possible. That inviting beautiful fire lit at the wrong time however could also become 50-foot flames that on hot windy summer days would roar towards our property and have my dad on the roof with a hose wetting the gutters and my mum, brother, and I, each with hoses, soaking our front and back lawns in a desperate attempt to stop our home being burned down. Our efforts, along with the heroic volunteer local fire brigade, meant that our house never succumbed to the bushfires that were a regular feature of my childhood.

I should make it clear; it was drilled into us kids that we must never light fires during the fire ban! But other people did, and they got out of control. And sometimes a stroke of lightning hitting a cinder-dry eucalyptus tree, its leaves loaded with deliciously pungent oil, would ignite an explosion and set off a chain reaction across the bush.

Fire has never scared me despite these early experiences. The flame of a candle, the tongues of a campfire, the curtain of a bush fire—it's all beautiful and invites awe and respect. It's no wonder that ultimately I would take up firedancing!

**Firedancing**
(Photo by Sasha Alexander)

# TRANSCENDENT

## FIREDANCING

Embodying the transformational element of Fire is something I have deeply explored as a firedancer.

I started firedancing in my forties. I was living on the island of St. Croix, in the US Virgin Islands, having moved there to start a new chapter working in aviation after living in Los Angeles and working in the entertainment industry for ten years (for the full disclosure read my autobiography, *The Naked Witch*—Rockpool Publishing, 2017).

As I worked forging a new career at the airport, I was drawn to the shows by the local fire troupe, Kiki and The Flaming Gypsies. I went to a workshop they held one weekend, and the rest became my new herstory to write! After a year of carrying gear, doing fire safety at shows, workshops, and endless practicing swinging *poi* around in my island kitchen and smacking myself in the head multiple times with them, as I dodged the giant centipedes that bolted out of the 200-year-old sandstone walls with unnerving speed, I was invited to join the troupe.

I would work at the airport by day and dance with fire at night. I loved its heat and the sound it would make as it roared around me as I used the different tools—*poi*, fans, snakes, hip belt and palms. I loved eating it. I loved gazing at it. I loved our fire community and the sisterhood we shared. I could arrive at a show feeling "burned out" from a long day at work and light up, feeling invigorated and restored again.

Some of my life's favorite memories are when Kiki, two other members and I would get in a plane, and I would fly us to another island to perform back-to-back shows on a weekend.

Ten years later, fire still fascinates and ignites my passion for life. I don't dance regularly in the troupe anymore—but Kiki is one of my closest friends, and when I return to the island, she always invites me to light up for a show for fun. Such a blessing!

To embark upon your own firedancing journey, research courses that are offered in your area. Start with somewhere close so you can regularly practice and get familiar. Practice with your tools unlit every day. Kiki is an occupational therapist and initially explored the use of *poi* for healing and coordination before it became a passion of fire and performance for her. You will find regular practice improves your coordination and balance—physically as well as emotionally.

When you are somewhat practiced and confident, consider attending a retreat—there are wonderful fire retreats around the world in places from Costa Rica to Ireland! Meet your international fire community and thrive.

I still firedance everywhere I can. On a recent trip to Las Vegas, I visited the Valley of Fire at sunset—a national park that was used as a set for the film *The Martian*—because it evokes the surface of Mars with its vibrant red rocks full of iron ore and many dramatic peaks.

Fiona Horne Firedancing at the Valley of Fire

I poured the Coleman's camp fuel I had brought with me (white gas and the cleanest burning fuel) into a dipping can (a steel paint can never used for paint), dipped my *poi*, spun off the excess fuel and lit up. It was so life-affirming as the fire roared around me and I danced alone amongst the rocks, bathed by the setting sun.

I still carry my *poi* everywhere with me—once you start dancing with fire, you can never stop!

## **CLIMB AN ACTIVE VOLCANO**

The first volcano I climbed was in Bali thirty-five years ago. I had travelled to the island alone to explore, and I was excited to experience sunrise from the top of Ganung (Mount) Batur. This was before it was popular with tourists the way it is now. I found a little *warung* (guest house) to stay in, run by a local family whose son would walk me and a couple of other people up the volcano in the morning.

At 3 a.m. there was a knock at the door. I had a thick jumper on as it was chilly. I had gone to sleep a few hours before in my clothes, ready to depart. The guide was wearing a t-shirt, shorts, and a pair of worn flip-flops. Off we set into the dark. As black as it was, he knew where to go and only occasionally swung a torch in an arc in front of him. I just followed the faint glow of his grubby white t-shirt ahead of me. We stopped at another *warung* and collected another couple who were American. Eventually, we were on a dirt trail leading up in the shadow of a large mountain.

We didn't speak much as the trail got really steep and I broke into a sweat, removing my jumper and tying it around my waist. Our guide bounded up the trail. I was amazed how he flew in his flimsy foot attire. At one point, we heard a crack and looked up to see red sparks shooting into the sky from the top of the mountain. We stopped twice to take a drink of water, but the pace was rapid, and we reached the summit by 5 a.m. The sky was starting to lighten and now we had a chance to catch our breath. The guide turned to me and said in broken English something that amounted to saying that he liked walking in the dark because it was easier to dodge lava and rocks. I said I did too!

The sunrise was so magnificent. Our guide served us warm cola in cans for a caffeine hit and warm eggs that he had cooked in the steam coming off the volcano.

I loved the walk back along the rim of Gunung Batur with steep ash promising a cushioned tumble if I slipped off the trail. Further away, dense flows of solidified lava served as ominous reminders of catastrophic eruptions that engulfed villages and temples in 1917 and 1926. Batur has erupted a number of times since—most recently in 2000.

The earth was warm from the churning activity going on underneath and I loved that this warmth was a potent, tangible reminder of the cauldron of creation, both metaphorically in our Witchcraft and literally at the center of our planet.

Another volcano I climbed is Mount Yasur on the island of Tanna in the Pacific Island country of Vanuatu. I travelled there in my early thirties and loved the mystical forces as revered by the ni-Vanuatu (the traditional name for the local people). There is also an island called Ambrym where there are two live volcanoes (or more accurately, one large one with two active calderas) and the locals believe that all magick comes from this island. But you cannot climb these—only witchdoctors brave the volcanoes, and it is believed they use the powers to turn themselves into sharks so they can swim to other islands where they become chickens and walk up on land to possess the souls of hapless residents!

The island of Tanna is far south in the island chain, and the live volcano there can be approached by a 4WD to within a couple of hundred meters of the rim. I walked across the parking lot (which is just a big dirt clearing) before reaching the edge of the rim, peering down into the crater and its red molten contents. The ground was hot and there were heavy whiffs of sulfur and hissing sounds that then sounded like they were being sucked back like an inhaled roar. Intermittently the ground would tremble and a fountain of fiery magma would shoot up with a loud crack, its sparks spreading across the sky like fireworks. Huge boulders spat out of the caldera as if they were marshmallows before rolling back down into the broiling depths. I stood there watching until the taste of sulfur in the back of my throat made me cough. I continued walking around to the west side of the central crater and I was alone peering into three smaller vents that took turns firing up rockets of liquid red rock and white smoke. Even all these years later, I can remember it like it was yesterday—the rotten egg gas smell of sulfur—and the way the base of my neck prickled with delight as the molten blood of Mother Earth leapt into the air.

I love volcanoes!

## POTENT

### FIREWALKING

Firewalking is on my bucket list, but I've only ever walked on fire accidentally (when I dropped my fan fire tools and then stood on them…not intentionally!). Whereas firedancing uses multiple tools and takes a long time to master, firewalking can be mastered in a weekend. It can feel very confronting to think of walking across hot coals. The self-mastery required to own the decision and take decisive steps that confront your perceived necessary boundaries of self-preservation can be extremely liberating and unleash and unlock levels and layers of your life and capabilities in far-reaching ways.

You can have the Anthony Robbins experience with a lot of screaming and yelling of encouragement from participants. Or something more soulful, in a spiritual setting.

Personally, I would prefer an introspective atmosphere to walk across a fire bed of red-hot burning coals with temperatures well above 500° Celsius (932 F).

Firewalking has been in existence for thousands of years. It originated as a ceremony for healing and as a religious custom. The first recorded firewalk took place in India during the Iron Age. It is recorded that two Brahmin priests competed to walk across hot coals and the priest who walked the furthest was acknowledged in the records.

In recent times, firewalking also has a therapeutic use. It has been widely accepted that firewalking helps people face their fears, focus their minds, and boost their confidence.

Everyone I know who has firewalked (including other firedancers) has said it is a beautiful, soul-enriching experience. And that when you complete your walk, you are exhilarated and on a high that resonates for days and ultimately impacts choices you make and actions you take for months after in an empowering and liberating way.

## EXPLORE THE CIRCLE OF FIRE

When I was working as a pilot in the Caribbean, there were sometimes really long flights between islands. One time I flew three businessmen from the British Virgin Islands all the way down to Saint Lucia. In my twin engine Aztec, the flight took 2 hours and 45 minutes—no toilet, no break, and no climate control. It was a good flight, but I couldn't wait to get out of the aircraft!

The men were considering buying a cruise ship that was anchored off the coast of Saint Lucia. While they had their meetings, I was craving to explore this stunning mountainous island I had never visited before, so I jumped in a local taxi and asked to be taken on a little tour.

The taxi driver asked if I would like to go to Sulphur Springs where you could drive into a volcano! Of course, I said yes!

We made our way along winding steep roads that skirted lush groves of cacao and avocado trees. At one point the driver stopped and opened his car door and picked up a fallen avocado the size of a football and handed it to me with a grin! After half an hour of the most spectacular views of the glistening turquoise blue ocean from our high vantage points, we reached a sign saying "Sulphur Springs" and as promised, the road led straight into the caldera. We parked and the driver stayed with the car and lit up a cigarette while I (still wearing my pilot's uniform) walked the path that skirted a large flat pool of steaming, bubbling mud before coming to landscaped gardens and the baths.

Sulphur Springs, Saint Lucia

This was the perfect solution for my stiff sore muscles and although a little underprepared (I had no swimsuit), I got into the mud in my black underwear and coated myself in thick, gray, soft slush. It was very hot and very soothing. After half an hour or so I stepped out and washed off under a surging waterfall. My skin felt like silk and my muscles like jelly.

The sulfur smell was strong, and I was inside a volcano—but it's considered a dormant volcano. It last erupted 200 years ago, and it is the only volcano in the world you can drive into! So, for the Potent level of Fire, I suggest you try strolling through geysers and taking a mud bath in the middle of a volcano!

Another wonderful way to connect with Fire in a potent way is to take the Yellowstone Circle of Fire tour. This is on my bucket list; I still have not made it to Yellowstone National Park—I will one day! Yellowstone isn't shaped like a traditional conical volcano, but it has the largest super-caldera on earth and, incredibly, half the geysers on the entire earth are here! There is also the unique and enchanted Valley of Volcanic Hoodoos—which are eroded towers of rock (not an ode to New Orleans' beloved southern Conjure Man, Hoodoo Sen Moise!).

Do some research and find volcanic activity near you to explore or take the plunge and go somewhere like Iceland where they have 130 volcanos…some active, some dormant, and some of the most stunning and soothing mud baths you will ever experience!

## PASSIONATE

### FIRE ON FILM

Passively watching bland content does not stimulate your brain, nor nourish your soul, nor is it something aligned with the Passionate level of extreme adventuring.

However, watching brilliantly produced films that inspire and excite, especially when they are passionately told documentaries about extraordinary people doing incredible things, deeply immersed in a particular element, *is* something that can supercharge your relationship with the element that the film is aligned with. The following suggestions are the kind of movie art that can change your life and light a fire in your heart.

> ### FIRE
>
> All the elements are embodied with qualities of change and transformation, but Fire particularly embodies the essence of change. It is such a potent, vibrant source of energy and can confer so much joy even as it can be so awe-inspiring and also scary! If we are in harmony with Fire, we experience the challenges in life as opportunities to learn. When I have had everything in my life burned down around me, metaphorically, I have always said, "I will rise like a phoenix from the flames." And I have. Fire teaches us to open our hearts. The heat of our heart, the blood in our veins…that is all Fire energy.
>
> If we are out of balance with our Fire energy, we can get fixated on feeling resentful, frustrated, and even find reasons to hate ourselves.
>
> The worst kind of hate is that which is directed to ourselves, and includes lack of self-love and poor self-esteem, depression, and anxiety. This can also be directed outward towards others and result in lack of trust of others, frustration with others, and intolerance of others.
>
> Physically, a classic sign of Fire imbalance can manifest as chest or heart pain or tension in the chest. So, if you are feeling this way, explore an extreme Fire adventure with the confidence that it won't only give you an amazing memory of

the event, it will also address other deeper layers within you.

After your Fire adventure, you may find that you love yourself a bit more, that you have set yourself free, that you feel more comfortable in your emotions and more balanced, and that you just simply feel stronger and more joyful.

When you feel this way on the inside, the outside world and your experience of it can change for the better too.

There are two passionate films by Werner Herzog, the master documentary filmmaker and one of my favorite filmmakers of all time, that invoke the extreme edges of the element of Fire in your living room like no other.

## The Fire Within: A Requiem for Katia and Maurice Krafft (2022)

Katia and Maurice were fearless volcanologists and explorers who were ultimately consumed by their passion on June 3, 1991, by a pyroclastic flow on Mount Unzen, in Japan. This movie is a beautiful requiem to them. The scenery is awe-inspiring, diving into the heart of the all-consuming, all-liberating power of Fire. You are taken on a journey of deep immersion with Fire as it manifests within the molten core of the planet and all its expressions on the surface.

## Into the Inferno (2016)

In this film, Herzog and volcanologist Clive Oppenheimer explore active volcanoes in Indonesia (Mount Sinabung), Iceland, North Korea, Ethiopia (Erta Ale), and Ambrym in Vanuatu! I love that this documentary explores our origins as a species and the relationship every culture has with Fire and volcanoes. The film is mysterious, beautiful, violent—and adventurous! Herzog is brilliant with his musical scores and storytelling. I always take note of the music credits at the end. I find his choices are often moving and transformative soundscapes to use in ritual and manifestation meditations.

## CAMPFIRES AND MORE

If you are dipping your toe into the energy of Fire, a great way to start is to learn to build and sustain a campfire. Learn about the properties of sparking and nurturing the flame, using your breath to conjure more power from the fire, and how to keep it burning.

Lighting candles in your home and being surrounded by many flickering buds of flame can also feel very empowering.

Also, why not attend a special performance that celebrates Fire? The original *Cirque de Soleil* (now rebirthed after briefly closing) puts on fiery performances that are evocative and moving. Seek out an experience that you know will fill you with wonder and awe. Witnessing the energies of Fire, great and small, will transform your life.

# ELEMENTAL INVOCATION: PELE
## Worship and Invocation of the Goddess Pele

Fire has played a pivotal role in the evolution of humanity, and we worship the power to create and destroy that Fire contains. In every culture and civilization there has arisen a powerful deity of Fire: the Norse Freya, the Greek Hestia, the Japanese Goddess of Mount Fuji, Konohanasakuya-hime, and the powerful ancient Egyptian mother born of the Eye of Ra—Sekhmet. There is Ra himself, one of the most important and highly respected Gods in all of creation, the Roman Vulcan, Greek Prometheus, and many more illustrious, radiant, and fiery divinities.

When asking for alignment with the actions of burning away

fear and resistance and invoking life-giving warmth and sustenance during extreme activities, the Hawaiian Goddess Pele appears in her powerful essence.

> **FORGED IN FIRE**
>
> Use lava rock and obsidian to show respect to all Fire Goddesses.
>
> A few pieces placed near your fireplace or around the base of your candle on your altar will show the Fire Goddesses you honor the divine gift of Fire and appreciate the benefits it brings.
>
> Wear or carry peridot when aligning with Fire energy on your adventures.

I have always been drawn to Dark Goddesses. Lilith was the patron Goddess of my first coven, and she resonated in my life powerfully as I navigated the creative and destructive energies of the entertainment industry—particularly Los Angeles in that first decade of the 00's when I made my living there.

And more recently, Sekhmet has imprinted upon me from my time in Egypt.

It is the Dark Goddess's thrilling and captivating ability to destroy and create that inspires me to trust in the confronting, difficult things in life, and allow destruction to play its role in the creation of my life. When invoking and honoring Pele, for protection and good favor as you embark on your extreme adventure of Fire, what we are destroying, our fear and reservations, are potent fertilizer for the seeds of freedom and personal growth planted during our experience.

I offer this ceremony of worship and blessing as an example of honoring a powerful Fire deity, and if you are drawn to invoking another Fire deity before you embark upon your extreme adventure, please do! Trust your instinct and innate connection to divine source.

### ESSENTIAL OILS TO ALIGN WITH FIRE

Cinnamon

Orange

Basil

Geranium

### FOR CONFIDENCE BEFORE A FIRE ADVENTURE

In a teaspoon of carrier oil like jojoba or sweet almond oil, place:

2 drops geranium

2 drops orange

1 drop basil

Mix and use a rollerball to anoint to the base of your neck and over your heart to invoke balanced Fire energy.

### BREATHING FIRE

To feel energized when embarking on a big Fire adventure, put two drops of cinnamon and one drop of orange on a cloth handkerchief or in an aromatherapy inhaler and breathe in deep before you climb the volcano, or pick up your fire *poi*!

Pele is the Hawaiian Volcano Goddess—and she commands deep respect. She is also known as *Ka wahine 'ai honua*, the woman who devours the earth, which gives a sense of her destructive power. Many look to Pele for protection.

In Hawaii, it's impossible to avoid the evidence of her power and generosity. Since 1983, her volcano has destroyed more than 100 structures on the Big Island—while adding more than 70 acres to the island's southern coastline.

Her forms are many, including the volcano, lava, and fire/flame. Pele can also shape-shift and will show herself as a beautiful young woman, a grand crone, and as a white dog. Some of her other symbols include the *'Ohi'a lehua*, a beautiful tree that quickly grows on fresh lava flows, lehua flowers, and the Hawaiian honey creeper bird which loves the nectar of the lehua blossoms.

Pele is considered to offer the gift of infinite love and is a powerful ally to those who desire to transcend fear and limitation.

There are many Native Hawaiian legends regarding Pele, but perhaps the most interesting is the legend that you must leave an offering or gift to Pele when visiting her home on the relentless Kilauea volcano. This must be done to keep her happy and protect your home and family from her unpredictable and destructive wrath of lava. According to ancient legends, Pele is often seen in human form as an older woman with long flowy white hair. If you see her, it is imperative that you greet her with the utmost respect and offer to help her, even if she declines. To get on her good side, it is said that you must visit her at Halema'uma'u Crater (which sits within the massive Kilauea caldera) with food and gifts of things that are of value to you.

Even tourists, when visiting Kilauea, will be encouraged to make offerings to Pele. It is said by the locals, "In order to truly please Pele—*aloha* is the way to go!"

## Meaning of *Aloha*

This word is used commonly as a simple greeting, but it also refers to a *force* that holds together existence. It is this deeper cultural and spiritual context that native Hawaiians use. When using the word "*aloha*" in honoring Pele, you are gifting her your acknowledgement that she has harnessed this *force* through her tremendous resilience.

To honor Pele, ignite your inner flame, and invoke the element of Fire, create your altar with:

- A picture of Pele, an erupting volcano, molten lava, or other powerful image of Fire

- A red, orange, or yellow candle

- Incense aligned with Pele (It is considered that she likes sweet, tropical things, so think coconut, pineapple, and a floral like frangipani [also called plumeria].)

- Pieces of peridot—this glistening green crystal is a volcanic gem formed in the deep fires of the earth on Hawaii and is treasured as the tears of Pele. Peridot is worn for greater influence and power.

It is important to offer a gift to Pele on your altar—consider red flowers evocative of Hawaii's endemic ʻōhiʻa lehua tree. These are the first trees to grow after an eruption, taking happy root in the ashes after a lava flow. The locals consider that the tree sparks a strong, inner fire that grows into a sense of rejoicing in life.

Light the candle and hold your hands out to the flame as you gaze at the image of Pele. And offer this invocation aloud:

*Aloha*
*Great Goddess of the Fire, Pele*
*I honor You Who Shapes Sacred Land*

*Your Volcano, the expression and
embodiment of Divine Creative Power*

*I honor your Flame of Passion and Fire of Purpose,*

*Witness my Desire to align with
your Profound Power*

*Burn away in me what is no longer needed*

*Clear the Path to my greatest potential*

*Bless me with your Dynamic Action
and Glowing Essence of Love*

*May I have always have passion for Life*

*and live to the fullest in service, a
channel for Divine Spirit*

*Aloha*

**Fire Eating**
(Photo by Sasha Alexander)

# WATER

Ah, the element of Water…it is the one closest to my heart. My astrological sign is Cancer and ever since I was born (actually when I was still in my mother's womb, suspended in liquid, my lungs full of liquid) I have felt completely at home when embraced by Water, especially the salty sea.

I do love lakes, rivers, and other bodies of water…but it is the ocean that always calls to me. And that is probably why I am offering more activities with this element than any of the others! (Notice I have left out jet skiing and other horrible noisy extreme activities that scare the fish.)

## TRANSCENDENT

### SCUBA DIVING

I learned to scuba dive when I was 20 years old, as soon as I had saved up enough money for the PADI open water course offered in my beachside home suburb at the time in Manly, Australia. I passed the course and bought all my own gear—BCD, wetsuit, mask, snorkel, fins, weight belt—all of it! And I was out in the ocean every weekend.

My very first dive was a one-on-one dive with an instructor named Malachy, in front of where I lived, a little cove called Fairy Bower. It was late in the afternoon when we got into the water. As I was instructed by Malachy with hand signals, I dropped down to my knees on the white sand bottom and slowly breathed. It was my first time breathing underwater and it felt confronting at first but quickly very comfortable and familiar. Which was probably a good thing because about 10 minutes into the dive, a shark appeared! I recognized it as a gray nurse shark, which is not aggressive. The instructor and I just kneeled on the bottom of the ocean as the beautiful shark swam around us in a graceful circle.

Marsa Shagra House Reef, Red Sea, Egypt

It was the second shark that appeared that gave more cause for concern, a big bronze whaler that darted back and forth towards us getting closer with every swish of its powerful tail. But I did not feel fear, only fascination. Bronze whalers are known to chase surfers in waves (they can be so aggressive), but this one eventually lost interest and swam away. Malachy had me demonstrate some dive skills, removing and replacing my regulator, purging it, and removing and replacing my mask. And then we slowly swam back to shore.

After I sat in my little apartment looking out the window down at the ocean where I had just been, and a lifetime love affair began in earnest.

With just 25 local dives under my weight belt, my first overseas diving trip was to Truk Lagoon (now called Chuuk Lagoon) in Micronesia to dive shipwrecks.

I went by myself and stayed with a group of divers from around the world, on the *SS Thorfinn* (still in operation all these years later), a liveaboard dive boat which was once a whaling ship. We dived four times a day. One of the first dives in the morning was to the *San Francisco Maru* and it is really deep for a recreational dive at 62 meters—203 feet!

The *San Francisco Maru* was a cargo ship originally part of the Japanese forces during World War II. Chuuk was a territory of Japan at that time, and the US launched an air strike and sunk most of the Japanese fleet that was based in the lagoon. It was considered a successful effort of the war, if we can call war efforts successful. But the outcome now is that Chuuk Lagoon is littered with wrecks and is a scuba diver's paradise, being considered the best wreck diving location in the world. It is also a viable and supportive economic activity for the region which the locals benefit from greatly in these modern times.

I was briefed that this would be a short dive time at the bottom, no more than 8 minutes max, and then it would be a two-hour decompression, slowly ascending. Ultimately, I would be very likely to run out of air and need to use auxiliary tanks that were hanging off the boat at 10 meters to complete the deco time.

This just sounded thrilling and exciting to me, and I couldn't wait to get in the water.

I felt great as I descended down through the first 50 feet in infinite blue over the ship and then the tops of two giant masts loomed up out of the deep. Shortly after, the ship herself loomed, giant and sitting upright on the bottom of the white sandy ocean floor.

*San Francisco Maru* is referred to by divers as the "Million Dollar Wreck" because it was (and still is) chock-full of expensive cargo including tanks, trucks, mines, ammunition, aircraft bombs, torpedoes, and depth charges.

As I dived through the ship there were lots of other regular life artifacts that reflected the crew's life aboard, including cups and saucers with the markings of the ship's owners, beer bottles, cooking utensils, medicine bottles, binoculars…and in the ship's hospital even a surgeon's table with surgical implements!

Overall, the *San Francisco Maru* is in very good shape considering it has been underwater since 1944. I loved going into the hull and seeing an original 1940's lorry (truck) parked in there!

During the two weeks in Chuuk Lagoon, I dived 14 wrecks including an airplane! The whole experience was fantastic and lit a fire in me that all these years later has led to over 900 dives in oceans and seas all over the world.

I prefer warm water but some of my favorite dives have been in the extreme cold! In January of 2023, I dived off the bottom of Australia in the great Southern Ocean at Brewer's Bay. This is an area filled with great whites and orcas, but I was in search of something much smaller—the leafy sea dragon, a very beautiful creature that captivates me with its fantastical appearance. They are bony fish in the same family as sea horses, but they are named after the dragons of Chinese legends and fairy tales. There is video on my Instagram page if you would like to see the footage of the time I shared in the ocean with this rare creature. My Instagram handle is: @captainfifi

## THE BENDS

The Bends is a deadly condition also known as decompression sickness that occurs in scuba divers when dissolved gases (mainly nitrogen) come out of solution in the bloodstream, forming gas bubbles in the circulation. It is caused by rapid changes in pressure during scuba diving (ascending too fast) and during flying within 24 hours after scuba diving.

An aircraft's cabin pressure is substantially less than normal atmospheric pressure. This means that the nitrogen in the body will release quicker than normal and as a result there is a much greater risk of getting decompression sickness. This is the primary reason why a diver cannot fly after scuba diving and must wait 12-24 hours depending on the altitude.

Symptoms of the bends are joint pain, fatigue, back pain, paralysis of the legs, and weakness or numbness of arms. They can come on in 15 minutes to 24 hours after a dive and a diver must get to a recompression chamber to be treated. The bubbles of nitrogen can cause complete paralysis by lodging in the spinal cord and even cause death. But with timely treatment a full recovery can be expected.

My passion to live in the Caribbean led to me diving a lot there—but more freediving than scuba diving as it turned out ultimately! I have dived Belize with whale sharks and dolphins, as well as

Malapascua with thresher sharks and hammerheads. I have dived mostly during the day, but often at night…you see the most extraordinary things scuttling along the bottom of the ocean under the single beam of a dive torch as the Great Mother's velvety blackness engulfs you. I made a video called "Alien Disco" of one of my night dives on the West End of my home island of Saint Croix. It's on my Instagram.

In all the years of diving, the secret I've learned is that in order to give yourself the best odds to see extraordinary things, you have to spend more time in the water! Unless you are quite lucky, it's the number of times you dive that leads you to the best experiences.

Like on one of my dives when the boat broke down in Belize after departing Placencia to Gladden Spit. I had taken myself to Belize for nine days. I had hoped to dive with whale sharks. They were migrating through the area and everyone else had seen them except me! This was the very last day I could dive. You have to allow 24 hours before getting on an airplane after diving to avoid getting the bends. I had dived five days in a row and not seen them. It was the 6th day and the boat I was on broke down within the marine park. It was four o'clock, and the park was closed so everyone else had left. The captain had put word out for another boat to bring another engine.

It was just me, two other people, and the dive master on the little semi-rigid outboard boat. The dive master said if we wanted, we could go in one last time as there were spare tanks on the boat.

I was waterlogged but I thought, "Fiona, one more time, just get in the water."

Low gray clouds had gathered in the sky above. Nearby Guatemala had a huge storm system going through the country and we were getting the edge of it. As I descended, the water was a little gray and gloomy. I focused on the hiss of the inhale of my breath and the slow gurgling bubbles of my exhale.

I felt very relaxed. I had accepted that if I didn't see whale sharks it was OK. I had still seen amazing things and I had a wonderful time in Belize; it's a beautiful country with warm, welcoming people.

Suddenly, something whizzed up beside me to my left which made me start! It was a huge snapper spiraling up through the water so fast it looked really unnatural. I realized that I had swum into an area dotted with fishing lines. The snapper was on the end of a hook being rapidly pulled up. I looked around and saw my dive buddies a few meters behind me facing in the opposite direction.

Even though it's a marine park, the locals are allowed to fish for sustenance.

I backed away from the fishing lines and turned around, swimming in the direction of my buddies. They were a fair way ahead of me and when I looked down to get orientated, I could not see the bottom of the ocean. Then I saw a white spot that was coming straight up at me. In the murky gloom I couldn't tell what it was. This spot looked very strange, and it was getting bigger and bigger quite fast! Suddenly, a beautiful big silver-gray dolphin appeared face first out of the dark green sea below me and arced backwards in front of me, just a meter away.

I realized I'd been looking at the tip of her nose as she came straight up from the depths towards me!

I marveled at her size and beauty, but she was only the opening act!

She darted off stage right, and as I turned my head to look straight ahead, from stage left a giant whale shark appeared in front of me! She was majestic, at least 40 feet long, slowly moving through the green, gray water—her body dotted with a thousand white spots. I just felt my heart explode with joy and then she swam towards me! I slowly backed away because I had been told that if I touched a whale shark the fine would be five thousand U.S. dollars. I hadn't even looked around to see if anyone was with me, but the thought occurred to me that I did not want to be liable for this. Plus, I generally don't touch things when I dive. I just try to look and appreciate.

So, I carefully backed away with minimal fin kicks and she just swam right up to me! It was like I was laying alongside her horizontally. I was so aware how short my body was compared to hers. I felt an astounding sense of serenity as I lay there floating midwater with her. She seemed content too as we slowly moved along together. I eventually sensed another person nearby. I looked over my shoulder and there was another diver. So, I slowly rose up over her and let the other divers share in her magnificence. In those days, we didn't have cameras like go pros. So, no one has any photos; it's just in my memory forever.

The moral of this story? Just always say yes and get back in the water!

Most recently, at the time of writing, I have dived in the south Red Sea in Egypt, near the border of Sudan. I'm more of a nature girl than a wreck girl and the deep southern Red Sea is astoundingly beautiful with untouched coral and magnificent sea life including a healthy offshore population of my favorite shark, the hammerhead!

The big liveaboard boats that clutter the Red Sea further north do not go this far south because of the political unrest with Sudan. The happy result of this is the ocean is mostly left alone. I accessed it by staying at a small eco lodge named Wadi Lahami and run by Red Sea Diving Safari, an eco-conscious operator who runs three all-inclusive dive lodges in this pristine part of the world.

So, do you feel that scuba could be for you? Look locally for where you could learn or consider making a special trip to a place like Bali or Cozumel, Mexico to learn. My Caribbean home island of St. Croix has a number of great dive shops where you can learn and/or improve your skills in just a week.

Most of the world learns to dive with PADI but there are a number of other scuba diving certification boards, like SSI and NAUI, so look at what's available in your local area and if you don't live near the ocean, that's not a deal breaker. I know several people who learned to dive in a quarry!

> **MEET YOURSELF IN EGYPT**
>
> I offer women-only bespoke spiritual adventures of Egypt that include mystical experiences on the land and in the sea. We explore the pyramids, tombs, and temples aligned with the Feminine Divine and with ceremony and ritual, yoga and meditation, clean food, and clear guidance. We sail the Nile in a traditional dahabeya (Arabic sailing boat), and finish with a Red Sea baptism with dolphins, hosted at Red Sea Diving Safari. We have special guest speakers to inspire and help us assimilate the cultural and spiritual lessons, dine with Bedouin women in the eastern desert, and finally have an astronomy lesson so that the stars can guide us home. All these activities are presented as low impact, humane, culturally respectful, and responsible activities.
>
> Visit www.fionahorne.com/egypt to learn more!

## FREEDIVING

When I was growing up and watching TV in the 80's there was a show called *Man from Atlantis* with Patrick Duffy. He would swim like a merman, and I wanted to be him! My parents had built a swimming pool in our backyard. It was heaven to me. The deep end was 2 meters (6 ½ feet), and I could dive down with my little body and feel the weight of the water on top of me and then swim back and forth along the bottom holding my breath five times!

My brother and I would have competitions to see who could stay underwater the longest. We would pin our arms to our sides and squeeze our legs together and flip our legs like a dolphin tail, which is how the man from Atlantis got around.

Later in life I was drawn to scuba diving as my preferred water activity until I moved to the Caribbean in 2013.

My new home, the island of St. Croix, has a magnificent pier on the West End. The Frederiksted Pier is 1,526 feet long and it is held up by 60 cement columns that are encrusted with vibrant hard and soft corals and surrounded by a million colorful critters, including seahorses and baby puffer fish. Weaving their way through the columns are schools of barracuda, thousands of fish, sea turtles, and the occasional shark. The first columns are at 20 feet of depth, and the ones at the end are 90 feet. I've dived to the bottom of them all, and I also know that if you swim northwest about 50 feet off the last one, you'll find 103 feet of depth at the bottom of the ocean there.

Freediving at Coki Beach in Saint Thomas, US Virgin Islands
(Photo by Dave MacVean)

My Instagram is covered with videos I've made of my time diving around the pier. It's endlessly fascinating and the sea life feels like family! There is an incredibly healthy population of hawksbill turtles; we commonly see the babies grow up to adults. There is a family of spotted eagle rays that glide around together in formation. Hiding in the rocks and some of the old cement pylons from the old pier that was destroyed in 1995 during Hurricane Marilyn, are octopuses and moray eels that have been given names by the local divers. It also serves as a cruise ship port but that has not deterred the proliferation of sea life there. The catastrophic double hurricanes of Irma and Maria in 2017 (that I survived on the neighboring island of St. Thomas) certainly hit the coral and the sea floor hard. But everything is recovering now, and it is one of my very favorite places to hold my breath in the world.

I was diving the pier for a couple of years before officially doing a course to learn to freedive. In 2015 I was so excited to see a Facebook group posted by a local freedive instructor. I immediately signed up, passed the level 1 PFI course, which saw me hold my breath for three minutes and 15 seconds, and dive comfortably to 50 feet.

Eight years later the instructor Rik and I are good mates and dive for fun every time I'm on the island. With him I've doubled my depth to just over 100 feet, but I definitely feel the calling to go deeper now and will be doing some more training after I finish writing this book! I will head back to the Red Sea where the conditions are optimal for freediving.

Scuba divers dive to look outside—freedivers dive to look within. There's only one thing I love more than floating face down in the sea far offshore with a snorkel in my mouth slowly breathing: it's when I draw in a last long smooth breath, take the snorkel out of my mouth, and dive down deep.

Gazing down into the infinite blue, I have heard the Great Mother say to me, "Come to me, let me hold you." When I release myself to her embrace, everything in life makes sense, everything is peaceful, and the perfect, present moment is infinite.

Freediving is not just about going deep; it's so much fun to hold your breath and dive in and around coral formations, wrecks, and piers! Without the large scuba gear and bubbles, you are a lot more unobtrusive underwater, and fish come closer to you and stay longer around you.

If you feel drawn to freediving, like scuba, you can do it pretty much anywhere. Warmer water and calmer seas make it easier though.

Freediving is like returning to the womb; there's a sense of coming home. And considering we all started life floating in fluid, our lungs full of fluid, that makes sense to me.

I have freedived in the Caribbean, the Red Sea, the great Southern Ocean, off Christmas Island (the tip of an ancient volcano in the middle of the Indian Ocean whose sides jut down to 5,000 feet just 100 feet offshore) and Ningaloo Reef in Western Australia. It's fascinating to explore the oceans of the world as a freediver. The freediving community is very supportive and tight knit. When I started freediving, it wasn't as popular as it is now. It's become one of the fastest growing recreational sports in the world, overtaking even scuba diving! So don't be nervous. Consider heading back into the womb and exploring your inner realms in a truly physical, plane-defying way.

I have dived in many places, but still want to see the cenotes of Mexico's Yucatán Peninsula; they are on my bucket list. It is an area of exceptionally unique, natural beauty, particularly when it comes to the cavernous cenotes (underground sinkholes). Friends I have who have dived in these natural sinkholes tell me it's an incredible experience, as is diving through the underground cave systems there. In Tulum there is a place called Dos Ojos ("Two Eyes") which is considered one of the planet's most beautiful underwater sites. Two nearby sinkholes are connected by a corridor that runs about 1,200 feet long. Natural light comes through the holes in columns and the visibility underwater is pristine. Next year!

## SAILING

I became a sailor after the double hurricanes of 2017. I bought a boat, a sweet 32-foot Bristol monohull with the original Ted Hood design. A real classic girl. It was a crash course in learning how to fix boats. Considering she had survived the two hurricanes tucked away in a hurricane hole on Saint John tied off to mangroves, she had a tremendous spirit. I took care of a few small maintenance things and then had my first sailing lesson in her. She was so fun to sail. She caught the wind and flew along like a bird…or maybe a flying fish!

I made a new friend, a girl who was a carpenter on boats, who said she knew how to sail, and I trusted that she did. We decided to take out my girl one sunny afternoon. There was a light breeze, and it was just going to be a *three-hour tour a three-hour tour*. (I write that as I sing the theme from *Gilligan's Island*.)

But this three-hour tour turned into a twelve-hour nightmare. The girl started out doing well enough sailing my boat across the channel. Our plan was to moor in a cove on a smaller offshore island. But she made a critical error in approaching a different bay with the wind behind us. I remember having my bush flying pilot's hat on and thinking we were taking a risk putting our nose into a cove where there was no "out" and the wind behind us and the surge pushing us towards the rocks.

It was my job to grab the rope of a red buoy ahead of us. I stood at the bow of the boat, leaning out with a big, hooked stick as we raced towards the red buoy. It was the last one and if we didn't catch it, we would be on the rocks. I was not having fun and there was no way I was going to miss that buoy. I managed to catch it with my hook and pull it in towards the boat. She left the cockpit and came to me, snatching the buoy rope from my hand and promptly dropping it! Back into the sea it went—and up onto the rocks we went! I saw them sticking up out of the water like jagged, black jaws of death. As the sun dropped low, I knew we were in trouble. As soon as the boat grazed them, I heard a splitting, tearing, squealing sound. It was awful. The girl dropped the main sail and tried to put the small 20 horsepower engine in reverse, but it was having little effect. The wind, the surge, and the sea were pushing us up onto the rocks and we were jammed. Eventually I was able to reach the Coast Guard on the radio and call a tow service. In the islands, these kinds of mishaps can happen fairly often with the number of tourists that come to sail.

We were towed off the rocks, but we guessed we were likely taking on some water somewhere, so we had the bilge pump running as we were towed into a boat yard. It was dark and with the boat in the boat yard where it was shallow enough that it would not sink if it did take on more water, I went home. The girl said she was sorry, but I could see she did not want to deal with the responsibility of what she'd done.

The lesson here when having an extreme adventure is, don't take anyone at their word! Make sure you get proof that they know what they are doing!

Ultimately, my little boat required a lot of fixing. This is when I heard that the word BOAT is actually an acronym and stands for "Break Out Another Thousand." Her hull was damaged along the bottom from going up on the rocks and water was leaking into the central water tank. I felt so guilty that she had survived two catastrophic hurricanes, but I take her out for a Sunday afternoon sail and almost destroy her. So, I spent the same amount of money it cost to buy her, and I had her hull fixed so that it was better than new. I repainted her interior, recovered her cushions, and cleaned her so that she was shiny and fresh as a daisy. I replaced some of the metal on the boat and got her a new sail bag (to store the main sail in when it came down). I did a smudging ceremony on her using a bundle of bush herbs from the island—sage, soursop, and lemongrass.

I asked for her forgiveness and said that I was going to let her go to someone who knew more about what they were doing.

I sold her quite quickly to a lovely young guy who was a sailing instructor and volunteered teaching kids how to sail on the weekend. He loved her and I know she went to a wonderful home.

There is a saying amongst sailors that the greatest day of your life is when you buy a boat only to be eclipsed by the day you sell her!

My sailing adventures continued after this, but only on other people's boats! I joined a small crew to sail a 32-foot Island Packet monohull through the Sea of Cortez. It was just me and the owner. Well, as far as humans go, also on board was a Labrador named Jib and two parrots whose names I can't remember.

I found this opportunity through an online crew acquisition site. Looking back, I can say I was taking a bit of a risk but I was so hungry to go out on the ocean and I learned a lot on this sailing trip. I learned how to run an efficient ship's galley and to be very, very frugal with water (which I'd already mastered while living on the islands, but on a boat you take it to another level).

The captain was a freediver also, and we took every opportunity to get in the freezing sea of Cortez, diving with sea lions in the most remote locations. It was truly an extraordinary three weeks. I asked if we could dock at Bahia de Los Angeles and the captain agreed to add it to the schedule. The last time I was in this beautiful idyllic bay and town was when I was a sick alcoholic, in 2011. I nearly drank myself to death here after the end of my marriage. To arrive on shore eight years sober was pure magic. I walked alone down the beach and did a ritual of gratitude. Gathering items like shells and stones, I made an offering, stacking them by the edge of the shore, saying a prayer of gratitude for the gifts of my sober life. As the water lapped further in, my offerings were swept out to the healing sea. I cried some tears and wiped them away with my fingers before placing them in the sea, offering my salted tears to merge with the Great Mother's salted womb.

Sailing Miami to Key West

When that experience in Baja came to an end, I answered another ad on the crew placement website. A few months later, I helped sail a 74-foot monohull from Miami down to Key West. When I met the captain, he seemed a little strange, but he was an ex-airline pilot and I thought he would be a balanced person. I soon realized that I had probably taken a big risk again to be alone on a boat out in the middle of the ocean with a stranger! But I dipped my hands in seawater and anointed the threshold of the door to my cabin as I muttered a protection spell so that he would not come in and bother me in the night.

Despite some odd things he said, he did not harass me. And we made it all the way to Key West and then I got off…fast.

My favorite memory from this trip was doing the night shift and sailing overnight from Miami. We split the shifts up into four hours each. When it was my turn, I put on the harness (essential in case you fall overboard as it keeps you tied to the boat) and set the course on autopilot. The wind was brisk and coming from a good direction; we were fully under sail. It was my job to look out for the lights of boats that could be traffic hazards (I only saw some far away), and hours went by as I slipped into a blissful love of oneness with the soft roar of the wind and the silky slush of the ocean as we surged along.

The moon was almost full, and I gazed up at her from the open rear of the cockpit. I realized there was a glow coming from beneath me and I turned around and looked behind us and there were cascading torrents of the brightest phosphorescent plankton in our wake! The motion of the boat slicing through the water activates these microscopic organisms. It looked like diamond sparks and fairy dust in thick swirls stretching meters behind the boat and it was mesmerizing.

I realized I was a Seawitch out on the ocean. The captain was asleep for the next four hours—I was free, having the most magical adventure. My eyes scanned the ocean as I leaned back against the rigging, the white sail tall and taut above my head and the moon and phosphorescence lighting up the sea. I had a set of mala beads in my hand. I did 540 mantras that night.

But after this trip I decided never to place myself alone with a man on a boat ever again!

Since then, I have gone sailing with friends who own boats and loved it. The idea of cruising around the world on a private vessel still enchants me…maybe one day!

## SURFING

I took up surfing at the age of 54. I had always been scared of it. I had tried a couple of times in my younger years, but I grew up in the era of *Puberty Blues*, living in the southern beach suburbs of Sydney during the 70's and early 80's. *Puberty Blues* is a very clever and funny book which was made into a film and a television series. If you want a classic dose of Aussie culture, take a look at it. It was a horrendous time of misogyny, bullying, and the idea that boys surf, but girls just go and buy them snacks from the milk bar when they come out of the water and gaze at them adoringly!

So, I shied away from surfing and just went and became a rock star instead. It gave me some vengeful pleasure a few years later, when I would see those tough surfie boys and girls who used to pick on me mercilessly standing in the front row at my shows moshing around and screaming "Fiona!"

During the COVID years, when I relocated back to Australia, the opportunity to learn to surf came about. This time I embraced it with relish. I decided to walk the talk and really do something that I was terrified of! I had the opportunity to be taught by my partner at the time, and he was an excellent surfer. The first day I caught a wave lying on my belly in the freezing cold water off the western coast of Australia that is notorious for great white sharks the size of Volkswagen buses. I didn't care what was in the water around me, I just loved the feeling so much! Over the following months I learned how to stand up just for a few seconds, but I had the bug.

Even though the water was freezing cold, I wanted to get in it as often as possible and catch a wave on my big foam beginner's board!

> **WHAT MAKES MAGICK HAPPEN?**
> You do! With your actions and intentions. Walking along a deserted beach, I spied a circle of conch shells radiating out in a spiral. I sat in the center, the glowing rays of the setting sun in my eyes and the warm evening breeze stroking my skin. I meditated on the sacred cycles of life, and as the sea rose and fell in gentle waves, I contemplated that everything, good and bad, comes and goes with perfect purpose. The pink of the conch shells and the white sand focused my thoughts on love and purity, and my gratitude for the miracle of this moment. And then I released my thoughts, closing my eyes and just being. As I felt waves of peace and bliss wash over me, I offered the blessings I felt to the ocean that she could carry them to every shore. When I opened my eyes, I saw the new moon glowing low in the sky. I knew my wish was granted. I smiled…and my friend snapped this picture. Life is good. Make space for spontaneous rituals of gratitude every day and your life will be magickal and blessed. (See Photo)

Eventually I was proficient enough to get an 11-foot Malibu. This is a hard board, which slid across the water with ease and made it easier to stand up, but then I started getting injured! The first thing that happened was getting dumped when I attempted to catch a big wave.

I got sucked down under the water as the board shot up in the air. When I came up, I collided with the board and the fin chopped against my foot! I got a nasty bruise that made it hard to walk for a week and impossible to stand on a board. The next injury was two months later when a wave broke on my back as I was pushing up with my arms to stand up and catch it to ride.

Finding a Circle of Conch Shells on a Beach in Anegada, BVI

It was a fairly small wave, but it managed to crack my right front rib against the board with the force that it dumped on me. I realized something had happened as a sharp pain tore through my side and I couldn't take a deep breath. I wanted to try and paddle back out and catch another wave, but I couldn't lie on my stomach anymore, so I went in and told my partner that I'd hurt myself.

You can't do much with a busted rib, so I just had to stay off my board for two months until I could lie on my stomach on a hard surface again. That wasn't fun, but as soon as I could I got back on the board and I kept surfing in the foamy little waves, loving it. Unfortunately, on land things were very difficult and bad with my partner and ultimately, I had to get away from him.

And that meant leaving my surfboard and that time of my life behind me.

I once saw a fantastic video on Instagram of a group of grannies surfing. They're like a tribe. They are all in their 80's and get out on the boards every morning. It is possible to surf without getting badly injured. I think I was just a bit unlucky, but there were also a bunch of things going on that were telling me I needed to get out of this relationship I was in.

At the same time, I'd suffered an attack by a dog when I was protecting our dingo.

A dingo is a wild Australian animal, considered an apex predator and highly capable of protecting itself. But this dingo had been domesticated at the age of 6 months, rescued as a pup after her mother was killed. I had booked workmen to come on the property and trim the palm trees. It is common practice in Western Australia for "tradies" to bring their dogs to work. When one of the workmen opened the gate, this giant dog burst in and went straight at the dingo who was sitting next to me as I stood in the house doorway. And she was caught unawares. It had her head in its mouth, when she screamed a terrible sound, and I didn't think twice. I grabbed her collar and punched the attacking dog in the head to get it off her.

In the process, I lost part of my right pinkie finger and the pads of my ring and middle fingers were damaged. I couldn't paddle the board then, and for some time I needed to keep my hand out of the water while it healed. There were lots of signs saying I needed to leave that life.

I was told by a healer a couple of months later as I dealt with the trauma and PTSD caused by the attack, that the ancient Mayans would take people with magical powers to the top of the pyramid and cut off the end of their right pinkie finger to mark them as a Witch. So, I decided that it was a good thing my finger had been bitten off. It was reminding me of my powers and that I had the ability to get away from this very difficult relationship.

Stand Up Paddle Boarding Saint Croix, USVI

## STAND UP PADDLE BOARDING (SUP)

Stand up paddle boarding, or SUP as the acronym goes, is a fantastic Water experience that can be as mellow or as extreme as you like. I've included it in the Transcendent section because it can give you access to the ocean in a way that is really integrative. I have paddle boarded on lakes, rivers, flat seas, and rough waters! My affinity lies with flat seas. I loved gliding along as the sun sat low in the sky on my island home. Standing on the board gives you a stunning perspective; you can look down in the water and see eagle rays flying through the ocean underneath you, turtles popping their head up for air, and little fish darting in amongst the coral.

One of my most magical paddle boarding experiences was in January 2020 in Bahia de Banderas, the beautiful big bay along which the city of Puerto Vallarta lies.

I was spending a week on a sailing boat there and I had my inflatable SUP board with my light carbon paddle which was super-efficient for long excursions. I was there because there were whales in the bay. In season, up to sixteen boats tear around chasing them for the tourists all day but finally that distraction was over. It was 5.30 p.m., and the sun was very low in the sky when I heard a "chuff" and saw a plume of water shoot up in the air just a few hundred feet from the boat. I quickly and quietly grabbed my paddle and, untying my board from the yacht, I made my way out in the direction of the plume. It kept disappearing and reappearing tantalizingly 100 feet in front of me as I slowly followed. Eventually, I realized I was out in the middle of the bay, very much alone, and the sun was kissing the edge of the horizon. I just had my bikini on and although it was a warm evening, I knew I couldn't chase this whale all the way out to sea. So, I just stopped paddling and sat down on my board.

I said: "Mother if it is your wish, she will come to me."

And I just sat there floating on the orange sea as the vibrant sun cast its color on it, the small waves making a sloshing sound when they came in contact with my board.

Suddenly, I heard a *whoosh* and I turned my head and there she was! The giant girth of this whale was three times the width of my board. As her head came out of the water, her blowhole was so big I couldn't have even put my arms around it. I felt nervous for a moment, but then there was a *pish* sound and a second little plume…her baby!

## DIVING ON LAND

Stimulate your mammalian dive reflex and experience the transcendental peace of freediving, without getting anything more than your face wet.

Humans are mammals and just like whales, dolphins, and even otters and beavers who need to conserve energy when underwater, humans have this ability too. Stimulating our physiological dive reflex slows down heart rate, calms our nervous system, and encourages a peaceful contented feeling.

In my book, *The Art of Witch* (2019, Rockpool Publishing) I suggest doing this every day to achieve a meditative state and also before ritual work.

## DIVING ON LAND MEDITATION

Fill a bowl with cool water; add ice cubes if you want a skin tightening experience as a bonus! Sit comfortably and breathe deeply and slowly for a couple of minutes, consciously relaxing.

Take a final deep breath, hold it, and place your face in the water for at least 30 seconds (I like doing this for 90 seconds—you will find your breath holding ability increases over time). Do this three times at the start of your day as a soothing meditation. If placing your face in water is not feasible, then a wet washcloth soaked in cold water can mimic the experience to a degree. Add a couple of drops of lavender to the water, lie back, place over your face, inhale, hold your breath, and relax.

I was so thrilled I couldn't breathe, and still a tiny bit nervous because she really was so big, but the energy was so peaceful and she had come to me. So, I just floated and looked at her and her baby as they swam under and in front of me. After a few minutes, they disappeared and then reappeared about 50 feet away; first the mother's big *whoosh* plume and then the babies little *pish*. The sky was now dark orange red, and I could see stars starting to appear above me and streaks of boat lights appearing across the water far away. The twinkling lights on land far away made me aware I needed to paddle back and so I did, calmly and slowly, yet again in awe of the magnificence of the ocean and our place on this planet and the opportunity to commune with Mother Nature.

With all the time you spend in the ocean, there will be surprises and gifts. Stand up paddle boarding is a wonderful experience that can suit a number of different fitness levels. If you really have balance issues that you don't think SUP will overcome (because it does teach you how to balance), then you could try the following activity…but warning! I found sit down kayaking more difficult than stand up paddle boarding!

## KAYAKING

I took up kayaking while living in the Caribbean. There was a deserted island across from where I lived, and it became my dream to kayak over to it. The passage of water was not the protected azure blue Caribbean Sea, but the more exposed wild and raw Atlantic Ocean—but I had to do it! That was a unique factor of St. Thomas, the island where I lived. These two mighty bodies of water skirted the island. There was even a place on the north end called "Mermaid's Chair" with a spit of sand that at high tide you could straddle—one foot in the Caribbean and the other in the Atlantic.

The white arc of sand of Hans Lollik Island beckoned enticingly every time I looked out my bedroom window. One day, I saw a kayak for sale on Craigslist and bought it. I started with smaller excursions off Magen's Beach. It was my local area and I got confident, my upper body strong enough that I decided it was time to make the crossing.

> ### ICE
> Oh my goodness it took a while for me to convince myself that I enjoyed getting in freezing cold water, or freezing cold anything! But in recent times I have been exploring the embracing, invigorating communion of extreme ice adventure. I'm still very much at the start of my journey doing this, but I can share that I have been to Alaska in the dark winter when the sun does not rise for more than a few hours a day, and experienced my first sub-zero temperatures in the snow, dog sledding along a frozen ancient river, and firedancing in minus 40-degree Fahrenheit weather. Added to my list is sleeping in a glacier in Iceland, and Wim Hoff style ice immersions at home…eventually! I have seen that you can scuba dive in Iceland between the tectonic plates in a dry suit. Silfra Gap is an underwater stroll through a 230-year-old rift between two continents. The waters are crystal-clear year-round, and you can contemplate the American and European continents joined here…and then as they are now after separating in an earthquake in 1789.
>
> I will add that to the list too. And take heart that I could go to a natural hot spring straight after! Iceland is renowned for them too!

Friday night I checked the weather for the following day, and it was going to be a calm day with low winds and a clear forecast. "I'm ready," I thought.

It's 8,000 feet or 2 ½ kilometers (1 ½ miles) one way, and as I set out at 8 a.m. with a large bottle of water, some fruit, a few muesli bars, and a beach towel in a dry bag in the storage port of my kayak, I felt pretty confident when I got to the island in just under an hour.

I spent an idyllic few hours relaxing and laying out in the sun and at 1 p.m. thought I better head back early in case the weather changed unexpectedly in the afternoon, which was not unheard of. I was halfway out across the Leeward Passage when the wind really picked up and the surge of the sea built to five feet. The sky went dark and suddenly, my fun day had become very confronting.

I realized that no matter how hard I paddled, I was not moving forward but being pushed out to sea. All I had to do was miss the Brass Islands and get shot out between them, and I would be lost in the Atlantic Ocean. Those two little islands were the last pieces of land before nothing but an endless dark green expanse of churning sea.

I was kayaking with a buddy, and this is an important point: while the purpose of my trip was a solo dream, I knew it would be very irresponsible if I set out on my own. And so, I had made the trip with a guy. We did our own thing but kept an eye on each other. He was farther ahead of me, being physically stronger and able to paddle harder. I yelled at him to keep going and if I didn't make it to get help! So, he pushed on ahead of me.

At one point, I realized I could not feel my arms and my stomach felt like I had been kicked; it was cramping from exertion. I knew I had to get a grip and focus before blind panic hit me, so I started chanting a mantra. With every stroke of the paddle, I said: YES I CAN—one word per stroke!

I needed an immediate goal—the shore was so far away, and the surge of the sea kept obliterating it, making me feel I was out in the middle of nowhere…which I sort of was. But I knew there was the island of St. Thomas and my destination, the calm of Mandahl Bay somewhere in front of me. And there was something else! I spotted a white buoy in the middle of the passage. It was halfway between me and the shoreline. I decided that I just had to make it that far. I could hang on to the buoy and my friend would get help.

I felt a surge of energy move through me, and where my arms had felt like they were falling off my shoulders, I could rotate them now with more vigor. But I could not feel my hands; they were just clamped around the paddle and completely numb. YES I CAN…I continued to paddle and at some point, I reached the buoy. It was an incredible feeling to hang onto it as the sea and wind surged around me. I realized it was likely attached to a lobster pot below. There would be no other reason for a buoy in the middle of the channel. My friend was far ahead of me, so I could stay there and wait. But I was soaking wet and freezing cold. My icy hands gripped the barnacle-encrusted rope of the buoy, the sharp edges of them cutting tiny slices into my hand, stinging sharply with the salt. Then I remembered Yemaya.

Yemaya is known as the Goddess of the Ocean in the area where I live by the Afro-Caribbean and Santeria-practicing local community. She is the most nurturing and loving of all the Orishas, which are the deities of the original Yoruba tradition brought to the islands by enslaved Africans in the 17th century. The Orishas are aligned with the elemental forces of nature. Yemaya is often depicted in images as a mermaid, but at other times in rituals I had experienced her as an amber honey-skinned woman with legs and feet and shells in her long dark hair that flowed over her body like strands of seaweed.

Out on the dark sea, hanging on to a buoy tied to a lobster pot, Yemaya came to me. I felt her strong, protective energy in the surge of the sea underneath me and her voice was carried on the wind whipping around my ears. She told me that I would be safe, that I would survive, that I would be wiser, and I would always be loved. A profound sense of peace moved through me and I was able to take a deep breath and my heartbeat slowed. Even the ocean seemed to calm down around me. I could think clearly. I could see clearly. And knowing that I was protected by her, I let go of the buoy and kept paddling towards the shore. Somehow it was easier and within a short amount of time I had entered a part of the passage that was more protected. I was able to pick up speed and my kayak started to glide forward with ease.

I managed to catch up with my friend. In the more protected bay, out of the worst of the wind, I was able to call out to him. He smiled when he turned and saw me. He was clearly very relieved that he was not going to have to call the Coast Guard! He looked shattered and exhausted though.

We both slowly pulled up onto the shore and weakly got out of the kayaks. A quick hug and we got busy with getting the kayaks on top of the car. The sun had set, and it gets dark very quickly in the Caribbean. We were in quite a remote area and wanted to make sure we could find the track to find our way out and back to the main road.

I didn't tell him that the Goddess Yemaya had rescued me. But ever since then, it is always her that speaks to me when I am in the sea. I made an offering to her before we left the bay. While he was tying the kayaks on the car, I walked down to the shore and reached into my skirt pocket, retrieving some sea glass I had collected earlier from the other island. I placed this into the husk of half a brown, weather-worn coconut that had washed up on the shore. I traced my name in the sand with my index finger, placed the coconut next to it, and thanked Yemaya for my safe passage.

## Adventure Witch Tip!
*Don't get fixated on an expected outcome—allow the Universe to surprise you.*

## TRUSTING THE EXPERIENCE

A big drawcard of scuba diving for me now (after having done over 900+ dives) is to commune with animals I never have before. So, while in the Red Sea, I invested in a private day on a bay with an experienced guide who guaranteed a dugong experience with 95% certainty.

Dugongs are related to manatees and are similar in appearance and behavior—though the dugong's tail is fluked like a whale's. Unlike manatees, which use freshwater areas, the dugong is strictly a marine mammal. They are also known as "sea cows," because they graze peacefully on sea grasses, and I had been following this particular one on Instagram for a while and was obsessed with how he snuffled his snout (like a short thick elephant's tail) deep into the sand as he ate, before pushing off and gliding away like the archetypal mermaid. It is one of four living species of the order *Sirenia*, which also includes three species of manatees. And we know what a Siren is!

95% was high enough for me to go for it and invest in this expensive trip. But I woke up that morning sick with a slight head cold, which is rare for me. I rarely get sick, but I had been travelling previously with a group and a woman was constantly sneezing and not covering her mouth on the tour bus—it was gross, and I did my best not to catch it, holding my breath after every explosion that left her mouth…until today.

But I decided to take some cold medicine and go anyway—I couldn't cancel at this late date. I met the guide, and in not shaking his hand, told him I was a little unwell; I would keep my distance, but hoped to dive with the dugong.

We geared up, I signed all the waivers, and off we went on a zodiac with the sky darkening overhead. After two hours of gliding around the bay in a speed boat we had seen nothing.

The azure blue skies of the day before, which revealed the sandy white bottom of the bay and against which the dugong would be easily spotted, were gone. Today was cloudy and gray and it was hard to see anything through the steely color of the water.

The guide was feeling bad and started to make apologies and I had a choice here: to either get stressed and resentful and disappointed…or let go with love. And so I said, "No worries, it's nature and there are no guarantees. I understand. I will still pay you, don't worry, and I won't write bad reviews or be disappointed!" In my mind I accepted that sometimes things don't work out…and it's ok.

He said, "Do you want to just go for a fun dive?" Because I had the head cold, I said "No, let's just keep looking." I thought I would only get in the water and try to dive if the dugong appeared…and if not, it'd be a bit of a blessing being unwell. All outcomes were accepted—no resistance. I would just flow—that was the lesson of the element of Water embracing me. And then my scanning eyes saw a dark shape…a fin! "Dolphins!" I pointed…and WHOOSH out of the water leapt…a dugong! Playing and swimming with five dolphins!

We quickly did the final stages of gearing up to dive as the dugong, a female, sped away…she was shy…but I took a chance and plunged my hand underwater, holding my GoPro, not knowing what I would film…and when I looked at the footage later, her sleek silvery mermaid shaped body had glided by underneath me, completely in frame.

We got in the water, and it must have been my adrenaline, but my nose was completely clear! I had no trouble equalizing and we dived with the friendliest wild dolphins I have ever met. There was a baby who just kept zooming in towards me. And they exhibited the most extraordinary behavior. They glided in on their bellies on the sandy bottom, like an underwater seaplane landing, and then just lay still there. I lay next to one eye to eye…they have deep souls.

The infamous dugong of Abu Dabbab
Bay, Marsa Alam, Red Sea, Egypt
(Photo by Mahmoud Iberahrm)

Then they would push off the sand with their nose. I think they were doing what they had learned from the dugong.

They all play together in this bay and the dugong will swim and bound around like it is a dolphin. The male dugong is slower, and he glides in and lies on his belly and presses his snout into the seagrass bed to feed…before using his snout to push off the bottom and head to another area…just like these dolphins were doing! After a beautiful 30 minutes playing with them up close and personal (I started lying in the sand and mimicking them when they pushed off with their nose and they loved that) they headed off and we finished our dive exploring some beautiful coral reef.

The moral of this story is…no I didn't dive with the dugong… but I did do something completely unique and exhilarating that gave me an extreme appreciation of the magnificence and magick of nature and the "out of time and space" brilliance of the underwater world. As a Witch, the experience reminded me that Mother Nature always has a surprise up her sleeve. And the extreme lesson I received as I merged with the element of water was to allow the flow of life to take me to the best and most appropriate experience with trust, love, and gratitude.

Two weeks later, I did dive with the friendly accommodating Instagram-famous male dugong! I went back to the area after a scuba dive and there he was! It was a beautiful sunny afternoon and I snorkelled with him up close and personal for half an hour. And I was blessed with some incredible GoPro footage.

**See videos of my adventure on my Instagram: @captainfifi**

# POTENT

## WATERFALLS

When I was fourteen, I was put in a school for gifted but troubled children (well that's what my report card described me as). Despite being expelled from my previous school for "showing off," I loved writing and in this school for my writing requirement, I wrote a piece about a waterfall, which scored me 100/100. I had only been near a large waterfall once in my life at that point—Fitzroy Falls in the Southern Highlands of New South Wales. I stood on a deck that jutted out over a cliff hundreds of feet high as the falls roared, pouring over the edge next to me, their spray dusting me in fine fresh mist. I felt consecrated, all stress, tension, and fear in my young life dissolved.

Communing with waterfalls is a beautiful way to refresh your spirit and excite your essence.

## STAND UNDER A WATERFALL

Christmas Island is an extinct volcano sticking up out of the Indian Ocean about 300 miles southeast of Java. It is a territory of Australia and yet a world of its own, with a multicultural human community which includes Chinese, Malay, Sikhs, and Australians. It is called Australia's Galapagos Island, famous for its millions of red crabs, completely unique to the island. After the first rainfall of the wet season the crabs march in their millions to the ocean to mate and spawn.

Christmas Island also has a waterfall at its center that is one-of-a-kind.

To reach it you wind your way through an enchanted forest of giant Tahitian chestnut trees, slow-moving giant blue crabs crawling around in the roots, before eventually reaching a flowing bubbling spring. You follow its path upstream along a raised walkway to arrive at a stunningly picturesque and energetically captivating waterfall that flows over a limestone cave, held by long roots of trees and patterned with moss.

The white person's name for this glorious place is Hughes Dale Waterfall. The local Chinese Buddhists believe it to be the centre of the earth's Water universe and regularly conduct ceremonies here.

I stood under it and let the water pour over me. I felt transported to a period outside of modern times that saw the island become a source of mining of phosphate in the 1900's. Prior to that no humans had ever settled on the island.

Christmas Island is very remote and getting there is an adventure in itself. If it is out of your reach, research any other waterfall you can stand under and make a pilgrimage there.

## BOAT UNDER THE IGUAZÚ FALLS (this is my bucket list item!)

South America's Iguazú Falls, located on the border of Brazil and Argentina, are a glorious cascade of over 200 soaring water columns, some over 270 feet high.

There are many walkways and decks to view them, but you can also get into an inflatable raft and sail directly under them. They are high-pressure falls, and the roar will literally vibrate any stagnant energy out of your core! And you are completely drenched. People have shared that it is like multiple bathtubs of water being doused on you—what a baptism!

# PASSIONATE

## AQUARIUMS

To explore an extreme adventure with Water in a passionate way, I would like to suggest that you try something that will really lift your heart. Because Water is emotion, and intensely pleasurable feelings can be as invigorating as intensely exciting ones! I remember loving walking through the aquarium at Mandalay Bay casino during my first visit to Las Vegas. There is a tunnel to walk through and the sharks and fish swim over you and beside you.

When I was on tour with my band, Def FX, in the 90's, we played a show in Northern California, and I took an afternoon to visit the Monterey Bay Aquarium. It was magnificent. Well-curated and spectacular in its variety. I have always sought out ways to commune with the ocean when I am landlocked for a while.

## UNDERWATER RESTAURANTS

Dubai has one of the most expensive restaurants in the world…which isn't that surprising, a lot of things in Dubai are the most expensive in the world…but this one has an excuse beyond incredible food and service. It's entirely underwater.

Ossiano, in the Atlantis Resort on the Palm, is romantic, luxurious, and fine dining on a Michelin star level. As you imbibe, sharks, stingrays, and fish glide over your table and around you.

The world's first underwater restaurant is Ithaa Undersea and is located on Rangali Island in the Maldives. What is even more unique about this underwater dining experience is that you are actually five meters (16 feet) below the surface of the Indian Ocean!

You can also eat below the surface of the ocean in Southern Norway, at the Snøhetta-designed gourmet restaurant Under. It's a very different ocean to the blue and balmy hue of the Indian Ocean where Ithaa Undersea is, being greener and with completely different sea life. I love the description featured on the restaurant's website…

>  *Half-sunken into the icy waters of Lindesnes, Under invites you to dine five meters below the surface. The panoramic view of the seabed offers a visual gateway to the sea and connects the guests to the wildlife outside. This provides you with an*

> *opportunity to take in the otherwise rarely seen marine ecosystem of the North Atlantic Ocean.*
>
> —Source: www.under.no

In the USA there are the popular aquarium chain restaurants, which while not being as extreme, definitely evoke the heart-lifting energy of ocean immersion in a nourishing way.

There are four of these restaurants located inside an aquarium. You can find them in Nashville Tennessee, Denver Colorado, and in Houston and Kemah Texas. The view includes hundreds of species of fish from all over the world.

Finally, the Sharks Underwater Grill at Orlando's SeaWorld shark experience is a bit more thrilling, as toothy sharks remind you to chew your food well!

At times, visiting aquariums, I have wondered if I am partaking in an environmentally conscious and respectful activity, considering the havoc wreaked on the world's oceans by humans. The aquariums that I have patronized, fortunately, have maintained a safe and supportive environment for the animals within.

## DIVE INTO WATER MOVIES

There are so many! Some of my favorites are the sailing epics, *Maiden Voyage* and *Kontiki*. The freediving classic, *The Big Blue*, and the scuba diving thriller, *The Deep*! Movies that are inspirational and motivational, watched with intention to experience the element highlighted on screen in a transformational way aren't just armchair fodder; they are heart and soul food!

## FLOAT TANKS

My first experience in a float tank was over 30 years ago. They were very new at the time in Australia, and I was hoping to experience a transcendental and spiritual breakthrough.

## WATER

When we are in the womb, floating in fluid, our lungs full of fluid, our intuition forms. We are born with an inner knowing. A sense of awareness that exists before the self-identifying ego is formed.

Over time we forget that we were born with this intuitive Water energy. We lose trust in the world, we lose trust in ourselves, fear is born. When we feel so much fear that it paralyzes us, then our elemental Water energy is out of balance.

Expressions of this can include panic attacks, depression, anxiety, fear of failure, and even addictions to work and feeling overwhelmed. Choosing to have an extreme Water adventure can reset this imbalance. It can reinstate our ability to trust and go with the flow, by purging the excess of fear and burning off the residue of emotional exhaustion.

Water can cleanse us, it can hold us, it can fortify us. When we gaze at a body of water, it helps us know that we can find peace and a sense of clarity and comfort just by being and remembering where it all started for us. In the womb.

Water always knows what to do, how to flow, when to be still, when to move. Trust this innate Water wisdom within. Know that you can access it just by remembering your beginning.

Blending some essential oils and keeping them on hand for emotional support is always a good idea too.

The tank lid was lifted by the assistant, and I stepped into the coffin-shaped vessel before crouching down and easing myself back to float in the thick salty water. It was the exact same temperature as my body. I immediately felt like I was suspended in space, except for the sting where the salty water came into contact with a scratch on my foot. The lid was closed and in the dark and the peace I floated away.

> **BLESSED BY THE SEA**
>
> If you go to the beach, gather seawater, and keep it in the fridge in a glass jar with a with a screw top lid. Seawater is very spiritually potent and when sprinkled on things it is particularly good at dispersing tension, negativity, and fear. Anoint your own feet with seawater when stepping out into your day to clear your path of obstacles and encourage good flow in all your affairs and activities.
>
> To keep your home safe, anoint the door and window frames with seawater.

I did experience a breakthrough. At the time, I was touring with my band, and it was a busy and stressful time punctuated by moments of huge exhilaration on stage in front of large audiences. I felt balanced when my hour in the tank was completed, signalled by some pleasant meditative music coming from a speaker inside.

The next time I got into a tank about three weeks later, I had dramatic kaleidoscopic visuals, almost like tripping on psilocybin. I did not feel as relaxed, but I definitely experienced an alternative reality that gave me perspective on some of the things I was going through in my everyday life.

Float tanks are very accessible now and offer an extreme opportunity to tap into a restorative state of consciousness.

### ESSENTIAL OILS TO ALIGN WITH WATER:

Chamomile

Sandalwood

Jasmine

Rose

Lavender

### MY FAVORITE BLEND FOR FLOATY PEACE

5 drops chamomile

3 drops lavender

3 drops sandalwood

In a base of ¼ cup of jojoba or almond oil

This works beautifully for self-massage, even just massaging your feet before bed in this mixture feels like you've taken a long cool soothing walk along the seashore.

### EMBRACING THE DEPTHS

Make a float tank at home by filling your bathtub with body temperature water and putting a kilo (about 2.2 pounds) of Epsom salt in it. Add the floaty peace essential oil mix, multiplying the oil drops by two each, and put a facecloth over your eyes for darkness.

There is an interesting old movie about something extraordinary that happens when a scientist gets in a float tank, 1980's *Altered States* starring William Hurt. I had not seen this movie when I first got in a tank, but when I did, I definitely think I found an element of truth to it! He taps into what he believes are stored genetic memories and is transformed in the process. I won't give more of it away than that...I recommend you watch it as a documentary on shape shifting!

> **Adventure Witch Tip!**
> Another great way to align your Water elemental energy is to put handfuls of sea salt crystals on the floor of your shower. Stand in the salt as you shower and it draws out excess tension, anxiety, fear, and other results of Water imbalance.

## SUNSET SAILS

Another passionate way to explore an extreme sense of joy in the Water element is to go sailing with someone else at the helm! Sunset sails combine the satisfying peace that occurs as our planet turns away from the part of the sky that the sun appears to be in, with the bliss of gliding on the ocean. Sailing at this time of the evening is beautiful anywhere, but the most magnificent water sunsets I ever saw were off the west end of my island home, St. Croix, in the US Virgin Islands. I wasn't on a sailing vessel; I was on my SUP board—half a mile offshore and bathed in fiery red light as eagle rays flipped their wings on the surface around me, and turtles popped their heads up to take a breath and a look too.

# ELEMENTAL INVOCATION: YEMAYA
## Honor the Goddess Yemaya

When Yemaya came to me during my near disaster open ocean

kayaking adventure, her energy was encouraging, supportive, and fortifying.

I offer the following ritual for you to be blessed by the essence of Yemaya when you explore the element of Water in an empowered and adventurous way.

Yemaya is the Yoruba Orisha of the sea. Her fearless energy confers a great sense of oneness with the ocean and evokes a sense of safety and confidence. Yemaya is often worshipped as a mermaid, but she is much more. She is the giver of life, as all life as we know on this planet emerged from the sea.

When you are rebirthing yourself in a Water adventure, Yemaya can bless you with new life.

Yemaya is not only the sea, she is also the way the sea behaves. Her patterns of flow reflect our human emotions and lives.

Sometimes the ocean ebbs and flows gently, soothing in its sounds and movements. Sometimes the ocean will surge and roar, waves colliding in a ferocious storm. At other times it is flat, still, and reflective.

The element of Water embodies all the feels in our lives and Yemaya embraces it all.

For this ritual, use coconut oil. When I made it back to the beach and saw the coconut shell, I sensed it would please her. The pieces of sea glass were jewels for her. But I have been told that she also loves pearls and any blue stones that evoke the ocean.

**Gather:**

¼ cup coconut oil

6 drops sandalwood oil

3 drops ylang ylang oil

Ylang Ylang grows on my island home, as do coconuts. Sandalwood was a valuable item of trade, transported by ships in the New World and is an appropriate offering to her.

Mix the oils in a small dish.

Make an altar to Yemaya. (Creating an ocean-themed altar connects you to her whether you live near the coastline or not.)

Use blue, white, and silver candles evocative of moonlight on the ocean.

Place assembled seashells (especially cowrie shells), sea glass, anything that comes from the sea, as well as pearls, blue chalcedony, and larimar (a revered stone in the Caribbean).

Procure 3 shiny copper pennies (this is traditional and was shared with me by a Yoruba Priestess).

Prepare a glass with sea salted water (or seawater itself).

Gather a palm frond or similar long leaf.

Procure a picture or statue of Yemaya—this may be an actual creation of her by an artist, or it may be an image that she speaks to you through. It may also be a creature of the sea that embodies her essence and that you feel drawn to intuitively.

Play ocean sounds as you perform this ritual of worship—Spotify, Pandora, and YouTube have evocative ocean sound playlists.

Anoint the three candles with the oil and place the three pennies at their bases as offerings to her.

Using the palm leaf, dip it into the sea water and lightly flick it over your altar, including your representation of Yemaya to bring her to life in your sacred space, and then over yourself and then around you in a circle in a sunwise direction (clockwise in the northern hemisphere and counterclockwise in the southern hemisphere).

Dip your fingers again in the oil and anoint the soles of your feet, palms of your hands, over your heart, and at the base of your neck—this is symbolic of being held by her, safe and supported when you embark on your elemental adventure.

Honor the Orisha with these words:

*Yemaya*

*You live in the storming sea and the endless reflection of the moon at night upon your calm waters,*

*May you hold me in your embrace as I honor your eternal source of life*

*You are the maiden of the sea, The great mother of the ocean*

*All its creatures are your children*

*I ask that I may join your tribe.*

*Please remove restraints of fear from my heart*

*So that I shall be free and my life restart*

*If it pleases you, may I float upon your starry sea*

*I honor thee, I honor thee*

Sense what feelings come over you now.

Write a description of your magickal adventure and picture its outcome supported by her.

Sense her free-flowing nature of expansive adventure as your spirit is liberated from fear.

Feel your heart lift as your emotions are charged with positive energy.

Feel your body grow strong and invigorated, ready for an elemental adventure.

When you feel fortified and in full appreciation of her awesomeness, and your reflection of it, thank the Great Mother and snuff the candles.

Anytime you wish to honor Yemaya, using a leaf or your fingers, splash your altar and yourself with the seawater, or salted water with a seashell placed in it.

# AIR

Air is the element that I have spent a lot of time consciously bonding and aligning with—flying airplanes, jumping out of them—and yet when I was growing up, I didn't like the wind. I felt it was unsettling. I felt vulnerable in it, distracted and blown apart.

As an adult, I became very drawn to it in my extreme adventures.

I love the feeling of opening the door of a plane and feeling that prop wash buffet against my body. Air now feels like clarity and confirmation to me. When I have gone through a difficult time in the physical world, I will find somewhere that is windy and picture the wind blowing through my body, through my cells and clearing out the pain, sadness, fear—whatever is weighing me down.

## TRANSCENDENT

### SKYDIVING

The first time I jumped out of an airplane was for my 40th birthday. My girlfriend Tara told me she was going to take me to a place called Taft, a two-hour drive from Los Angeles where I lived at the time. We tore up the freeway in her little red mini and turned up at a desolate airport at 4:00 p.m. The sun was low in the sky, but my energy was high! So excited! Not really scared! I was strapped to the chest of a lovely guy after donning a thick pair of overalls and getting a lesson on how to arch my back with my arms and legs extended (the position I needed to assume and maintain once I was out of the airplane and plummeting through the sky) and then it was off in a small Cessna 172 airplane.

We climbed to 10,500 feet. There is a video of Tara about to jump and she shrinks away from the door and then there's me leaning out enthusiastically with a smile on my face.

Jumping The Boneanza Boogie at Skydive Elsinore
(Photo by Montana Powell)

It was the best feeling ever and I was hooked.

That night we went to the actress Demi Moore's daughter's birthday party. Her name is Rumer and her best friends Lindsay Lohan, Paris Hilton, and her dad Bruce Willis were there, along with her mum and partner at the time, Ashton Kutcher. It was a celebrity-soaked night, and yet I couldn't stop thinking about jumping out of that little airplane in that little town, three hours before.

From then, I drove up to Taft every weekend and completed the eight levels of the Accelerated Free Fall (AFF) program. I did my first twenty jumps at my (now home) drop zone of Taft as you are required by the US Parachutist Association for the official accredited skydiving student program.

And then I proceeded to jump out of airplanes all over America and all over the world.

Skydiving is one of the most thrilling and exhilarating sports.

The community of skydivers is close and supportive like no other. Probably because we all come so close to injury and death so often—every skydiver knows someone that's broken their femur and someone who has died.

But it's still worth it all. As we cry out before we jump, "Blue Skies! Black Death, we're all going to die! But not today!" we accept the risk and take the leap of faith…sometimes twelve times in one day if the weather's good and the loads are going up!

I reached 498 jumps in Dubai in 2016, and that's the last time I've jumped for now. My final view under canopy that day was of camels trekking through the desert below me and their long shadows across the sand in the setting sun. Later that year, I became a commercial pilot and focused on flying the airplane rather than jumping out of it!

I advise that to align with Air in this way, go and have a tandem jump to whet your appetite. I actually did five tandem jumps before I committed to the AFF; I was nervous I wouldn't be able to steer the canopy and flare it on landing. So, I kept letting someone else do it for me. Interesting to think that ten years later I became a commercial pilot and flared and landed an airplane for my passengers all the time! I definitely got over my fear of landing anything airborne!

Is it better to tandem jump over the pyramids or over your local drop zone? Both are amazing—in fact, every jump anywhere is amazing. There is nothing like taking an "air bath" to clear your head and clear your soul.

Contact your local drop zone (just look it up online and book your jump) and then, if you are like me, you will go and complete the AFF program and always be glad that you did.

## FLYING ECONOMY

Where to jump? Do we hunger for the extreme of the extreme…can we afford it?

Jumping off an AS350 B3 chopper from the height of 23,000 feet, just below Everest, and landing at the Himalayan paradise of Syangboche (12,340 ft) and Amadablam Basecamp (15,000 ft) is easily one of the most thrilling aerial adventures in the world. The adrenaline rush, the eye-feasting view of the picturesque Sherpa settlement, the backdrop of the world's highest peak, Mt. Everest, along with other equally petrifying sister peaks, and the whole alpine experience…what else can an extreme adventure seeker dream in a lifetime?

This amazing once in a lifetime experience is $25,000 USD.

It's worth it—chartering the plane, the cost of the fuel, the safety, the special gear, the insurance, it all adds up quickly! But can you afford it? I can't right now, that's for sure!

It also costs a lot to jump out over the pyramids of Giza—same deal, chartering the plane, the fuel, the clearances, the insurance…a tandem for one is $11,500 and includes a private hotel room and two skydives. The people you are getting strapped to (the tandem masters) get a fraction of this fee so you will need to tip large too.

But there are incredible experiences to be had for much less. That last jump I did in Dubai cost $25 US dollars (for the jump ticket—i.e., the seat on the plane) but you have to factor in the cost of all my training and gear which would have added up over the years. A tandem skydive usually costs between $250 - $400 US dollars, depending on where you are in the world.

I skydived into the Blue Hole in Belize as part of the Boogie in Belize that I attended three years in a row when I was jumping a lot. It was truly mind and heart blowing to get out of the airplane at 13,500 feet, in bare feet, ready for your splashdown landing.

Straight after we took off our skydiving gear and scuba dived the Blue Hole with its lurking sharks and giant limestone stalactites and columns—the perfect combo of extreme Air and Water.

That whole trip was $3,000 USD. Don't let money squash your dreams. Save up for something special—you're worth it! And find the adventure that fits you. I have often found that when I love something I just go and get a job doing it or find a job in a supportive role for the activity. When I became a marketing manager for an aviation company so that I could be closer to airplanes and the industry, I ended up managing the flight school, flying the scenic tours, and saving up to become a commercial pilot. It was also during this job that I put together two aid missions to Haiti, securing donations of money, food, fuel, and aircraft—and got to fly those too. Where there is a will there is a way to merge with your chosen element.

Recently I was having dinner with a high-powered real estate broker in Dubai and she told me about a team-building meeting they had where they jumped out of airplanes. They went to Skydive

Dubai at the Palm, an infamous man-made island in the shape of a palm tree. The drop zone is in the center of the trunk, and you approach over the water to land on the short runway. I know because I have flown that plane from the right seat and been on the controls under dual instruction on approach and landing. She said everyone had to do it and everyone was scared—but she loved it. She said she felt blissful, all her past baggage left behind.

She took a leap of faith into the future. She said, "It shifts something in you, plunging out into the unknowable of air—you can't see it, but you can feel it rushing past your skin, cleaning your aura." We skydivers call it taking an air bath.

The broker went on to say jumping shifted some blocks for everyone who participated. Two of her teammates landed and found out two difficult deals they were trying to close…just did! Their energy and levels of success were transformed after the jump.

## **FLYING AIRPLANES**

I used to love being a passenger in airplanes, but I would always look wistfully towards the left when I boarded an aircraft, towards the cockpit, wishing that I was up there flying the plane and not just flying in it.

I got my private pilot certificate in Bakersfield California, in May of 2013—I was 47.

After working in the entertainment industry and being based in Los Angeles for eight years, I met the love of my life when I took up skydiving at the age of 40. He was a fantastic skydiver and a commercial pilot and flight instructor. We spent many happy days at the airport in Bakersfield, his hometown. We were together for five years and married two of them, but the marriage ended painfully in 2011. Getting my private pilot's license was therapy. I hoped to rebuild my life in the Caribbean. It had been a dream of mine since I'd been a little girl to visit the blue, blue waters and green islands of that part of the world but growing up on the other side of the world in Australia I didn't know how I would ever get there as a tourist let alone to ultimately live and work there one day!

Captain of an Aztec PA23, for private air charter company

So, when our marriage ended, I completed my private pilot training and passed my check ride. I went to Hollywood Tattoos on Cahuenga and got a propeller of a 1934 Stearman biplane tattooed on my left forearm. I had one suitcase, a credit card, a broken heart, and a dream. I left California and planted myself on the island of Saint Croix, in the US Virgin Islands. I had a friend that worked there as a pilot, and she was my launching point and cheer squad. I started going to the airport every day and bothering a private charter operator and fueler called Bohlke International Airways for a job. The full story of how I became a commercial pilot, volunteered, coordinated, and flew two humanitarian aid missions to Haiti, and ultimately became the most requested captain for the on-demand charter airline I flew for is in my autobiography, *The Naked Witch*, published in 2017 by Rockpool Publishing.

On my Patreon page, I'm reading my autobiography on video and adding extra anecdotes and behind the scenes reveals. If you would like me to read my autobiography to you, please check out my Patreon page! www.patreon.com/fionahorne

### AEROBATIC FLIGHT IN A JET FIGHTER

I've recommended aerobatic flights, and you can go up for a 45-minute introductory aerobatic flight in smaller piston tailwheel aircraft at a number of airports, but what about in a jet fighter? Seriously, when I was writing this book, I found this option online offered in Los Angeles and I was like "Oh my Goddess, I have to do this!" So, if you do it before me let me know what it's like. Otherwise, I'll put my experience on my socials! It's $6,500 for a 45-minute flight—so might need to save up for it first!

Be sure to make offerings to Mercury, the Roman God of speed and flying, and ask for his blessings before you embark on this magickal adventure!

Be a real-life Top Gun! Maybe it's just me, but I love this stuff—not that these planes were designed for war, but for the fact they are extraordinary flying machines. I would get on an alien spaceship with equal enthusiasm if it flew like these things do! Actually, I would get on an alien spaceship with enthusiasm no matter how it flew! Here is the scoop on this experience…indulge me! Or maybe you are an aviation

> geek like me and will get a thrill just reading it!
>
> *"Adrenaline's Fighter Jet Rides Los Angeles are truly a white-knuckle adventure which gives you the rare opportunity to fly a real fighter jet, an L-39 Albatross.*
>
> *This white-knuckle adventure gives you the rare opportunity to fly a fighter jet. That's right—you're not just along for the ride…With this experience, you actually get to man an L-39 Albatross just outside of LA!*
>
> *To begin the journey, a highly decorated veteran pilot gives you a fascinating history of the aircraft (it's still in use today for military exercises). After learning the nuts and bolts, you're geared up and seated in the tandem cockpit. Your heart races as your co-pilot takes off with powerful acceleration—this ain't no commercial aircraft!*
>
> *Above the clouds, your flying buddy breaks down a few hair-raising maneuvers and then lets you take over the yoke. You'll learn several air combat tactics such as the split-s and loops. These are actual maneuvers from actual military training programs—everything on this flight is the real deal!"*
> Source: https://www.adrenaline.com

The journey to becoming a commercial pilot took four years and at one point I was working four jobs: hosting a breakfast radio show from 5:00 a.m. till 9:00 a.m., then going to the airport and working as a marketing manager in the office from 10:00 a.m. to 7:00 p.m., then going to firedance at a resort until 10:00 p.m. and then going to bed, doing the social media for my employer, passing out at midnight to get up and do it again the next morning! Add teaching yoga on the weekend and it took me three years like this to save up money for commercial flight school.

But I got there and returned to Los Angeles in 2016 for my training and then went back to the islands and worked as a commercial pilot from November 2016 through March 2020 when COVID shut it all down.

I ended up going back to Australia during the COVID years and became a rock star again, playing guitar and singing in a band called Seawitch! But that's another story!

At the time of writing, I am nomadic and have not picked up flying again as a full-time career. But I can and no doubt will at some point.

If you want to fly an airplane, you don't have to make the massive commitment of becoming a student pilot, private pilot, or even a commercial pilot. Any airport that has a flight school will offer introductory flights where you can sit in the left seat and fly the airplane while the instructor is in the right seat, as you fly under dual instruction.

I flew my first 100 hours in a Citabria Decathlon aerobatic plane that was owned by my partner at the time and his father. I was very lucky to get the hours in the aircraft that I did, flying under dual instruction, because my partner was an instructor. I flew loops, hammer heads, stalls, spins…it was a great way to start my journey of flight and to understand how to recover from unusual attitudes!

All the pilots will know what I mean by that!

There are a number of different licenses: the sport pilot category is a great option if you're looking to fly small planes recreationally. There are certain criteria: you can only have one passenger, the plane can't weigh more than 1,200 pounds fully loaded, nor exceed a speed of 120 mph, and you can't fly at night or in inclement weather (needs to be VFR minimums—this stands for Visual Flight Rules). But it's a great option for people who want to fly a plane on the weekend for fun and take a friend for a $100 hamburger! That's code for flying from one airport to another and eating at the restaurant there. The majority of that $100 is for aviation fuel!

Anyone that has more questions about becoming a pilot, please email me. I'd be happy to share more about my journey and maybe I can give you some tips in the right direction. You can email me at fi@fionahorne.com.

## POTENT

### HOT AIR BALLOONING

The first hot air balloon ride I ever did that I didn't jump out of was in Egypt, two months ago from the time of writing this book. From the river cruise boat I was staying on, I took a small ferry across the Nile to be picked up by a car and taken to a large field. It was very dry, very dusty, and in the darkness. The roaring fires of thirty hot air balloons being inflated from lying like giant silk blankets on the ground to pristine luminous orbs of floating potential is something I will never forget.

Mounted above the balloon basket and centered in the mouth of the balloon is the "burner," which injects a flame into the envelope, heating the air within. And hot air rises! All the passengers were instructed to clamor into the baskets according to weight and hang on! There was also a good safety briefing before the men holding the baskets let go and we floated up into the air!

The pilot of the balloon was very adept and managed to work with the prevailing breezes to float us low over a recently excavated temple. We drifted silently except for the woosh and bubbling roar of fire igniting as the pilot filled the balloon with hot air from the burner at the center of the basket above his head. I just felt deliriously happy gazing across the lush green fields of Luxor as the sun crept into the sky—a giant milky red ball low on the horizon signaling a hot day was ahead, but right now the only heat was coming from above our heads and the balloon.

View of Luxor, Egypt from a Hot Air Balloon! (Photo by Author)

As the propane gas cylinders emptied it was time to touchdown. We landed perfectly in the desert with local village kids running to catch the basket and keep it upright as we glided in. Thank you Beyond Horizon Balloons for an excellent experience!

The other balloons I've flown in (that I've jumped out of) were once over Arizona and once over inland California.

A sunrise hot air balloon is fabulous anywhere and a beautiful affirmation of the origins of flight for humans. Ride in one and you will experience a supreme sense of serenity and surrender to the blissful empowering element of Air.

### BALLOON BUCKET LIST

A hot air balloon ride over central Turkey's Cappadocia region is my absolute bucket list experience! Rising aloft to 1500 feet provides 360-degree views of the enchanted limestone spires and "fairy chimneys"—something you can't see at ground level. Kapadokya Balloons is the first company that introduced hot air balloon tourism in Cappadocia.

I will be planning to take a magickal adventure group with me here in 2025. If you would like to come with me, email me at fi@fionahorne.com to receive all the information about how we will explore the deep ancient energy and vibrant creativity of Turkey…and have the magickal adventure of a lifetime!

## INDOOR SKYDIVING

I got really serious about indoor skydiving when I got really serious about trying to get a world record in skydiving.

I had about 300 jumps and most of them were on my belly—I had not mastered the art of head down freeflying. I could "sit fly" which looks like you're sitting in an armchair in the sky. I loved flying in sit and then elongating one leg to make me spin on the spot as I hurtled through the air at 120 miles an hour before going to my belly to pull the pilot chute handle and release my parachute.

> **HOW DOES INDOOR SKYDIVING WORK?**
> A powerful vertical wind tunnel keeps you suspended in a simulated skydive, before allowing you to gradually descend in a controlled way.
>
> The air blows upward at 270 km/h (168 mph) and allows the flyer to defy gravity and perform skills, like turns and flips and sit flying.
>
> Wind is created using powerful fans or turbines that draw in air from the surrounding environment and accelerate it through the tunnel at high speeds. This creates a smooth flow of air that simulates the experience of freefalling through the sky.
>
> Thanks to these wind tunnels that are so popular now, the dream of flying without wings and without jumping out of an airplane or off the top of a mountain is possible! You soar up to four meters above the net and sometimes even higher when you are more experienced. I love being at the top of the tunnel and looking down. You cup the air like you're arching your body forward and catch the wind with your belly, and it pops you up to the top. Then to come down you arch hard and float back down. You literally learn how to fly your body in the tunnel. To turn to the right, you drop your

right arm a little and look over your right shoulder and to turn to the left you drop your left arm a little and look over your left shoulder.

You have to stay relaxed, but you also have to fly your body—it's an exhilarating skill that everyone can do if you are reasonably fit. Children are really good at it! They don't have any fear and their little bodies are like strong jelly! So supple and flexible they fly like crazy fairies in there!

These machines cost $500,000. So don't be surprised that four minutes costs a solo flyer $80 on average—it's worth it! It gets cheaper if you fly with other people at the same time—you all just split the cost of the "tunnel time." There are limits to how many can go in based on how experienced you are and there are also instructors in there too to assist and teach you if you need them.

Your sensation of time changes when you're flying—one minute feels like a long time. When I was practicing maneuvers for the record, we would fly for three minutes sometimes, and your body gets really tired! Remember, in a regular skydive the freefall is only a minute or even less from a height of 12,500 feet, the average altitude that most drop zones offer.

But head down flying I just couldn't get the swing of, so I started training in the tunnel to learn how to head down fly. The tunnel is a training tool that a lot of elite skydivers use and so do a lot of everyday skydivers like me.

It's tons of fun, and so good for building experience. The average freefall out of an airplane is one minute, but when you're in the tunnel you can fly for two or three minutes! It does get tiring, but you don't have the long flight up in the plane or the parachute ride down. You can maximize your flying time.

> **AIR**
>
> The Air element, when explored in extreme activity, is all about taking in and letting go. Air is aligned with our minds and creative thought, so when you face it and embrace it the death of all that we think we are occurs and we can enter into an experience of our true and free state. This element, when explored through extreme activity, is a powerful affirmation of all we desire to be and fueled by what we already are.
>
> When the element of Air is in balance within us, we can inhale and exhale fully, and in all areas of our being sense the trust that comes when we know that, just like the next breath will come and go, so will feelings and emotions come and go, and we can trust everything is happening for a divine reason. We trust in the flow of life, like the flow of breath (which is why I love yoga and freediving so much, because they are all about the flow of breath, but they are Spirit and Water extreme adventures respectively in this book).
>
> When Air is imbalanced within us, we feel grief, and lack of trust in letting go. Physically, this is expressed as shallow breathing, fatigue, lots of sighing, and a general lack of vitality.
>
> So, if you feel like this, it's time to face the Air!

There are I-Fly tunnels all around the world now. I would definitely recommend experiencing them to get a sense of what it's like to fly and be free! That column of air that roars up to float you is one of the most extreme expressions of empowering elemental Air that you can safely feel.

You might get hooked and become a world record holding tunnel flyer! It has become a sport in itself!

My world record did happen. It was a head down formation flown by thirteen of us over the skies of Washington State in 2010.

What made it a world record was that we were all over the age of 40 and it was the first time our demographic had flown head down in this sized group in a formation. We achieved it on our fifth attempt. The plane had climbed to 14,000 feet to give us a little more time in freefall to create our formation. We had to fly in specific slots and dock with our hand grips exactly as designated successfully. We were on oxygen on the way up and when you remove those tubes from your nostrils and go to the door of the airplane in your designated position, the feeling of excitement and also fear of failure is very palpable—it was for me anyway! A wonderful and very experienced skydiver, Bruce McElfish, who had the most serene blue eyes and was flying in the slot directly opposite me, just smiled at me and nodded a single nod as we were perched in the doorway, and I knew that we could do this.

Five of us left the aircraft at once and formed the base of the formation in a circle as the other jumpers dived out behind us. Upside down through the air at 180 mph we hurtled, feeling so peaceful. The other skydivers flew in and took their docks. When the last one joined, you could feel the energy ripple through our formation like electricity.

It was the most incredible sensation! We had it! Bruce and I had not unlocked our eyes since we left the plane, he was my anchor, but now it was time to break away. We had reached our hard deck (the lowest altitude before it's mandatory to open your canopy—on this jump it was 2,500 feet). It was my job to stay in place and let everyone fly away from me. We let our hands go, and as everyone turned and flew away on their heads, I went to my belly, did a barrel roll to check that no one was above me and "waved off" (this is waving our arms over our head to show any other skydivers around that we plan to open our canopy). My canopy opened beautifully and as it arced above my head and I reached up to grab the risers to fly it, I let out a howl of joy!

When we landed, all the jumpers were looking at each other with smiles, but we had to wait until the official review of the image taken of the formation by the camera flyer. It was put on the big screen and carefully reviewed by the officials…and approved! We had the record!

Sitting here now typing this my hair stands up remembering just how amazing it felt. What made it even more amazing was that during the first four attempts I did not fly well. I was the least experienced out of all the skydivers. I was messing up the formation. They were going to cut me if I couldn't get the 5th jump right. I was so nervous and so scared of letting everyone down. But it was Bruce's clear, cool calm eyes that got me through. Bruce died a few years ago from cancer. His loved ones, and the skydiving community, will never forget him…and I won't either.

## ZIPLINE MAGIC

### Dubai

Fly through the middle of the city in Dubai on the world's longest zipline—yes! This is epic! It is the world's longest urban zipline at one kilometer (just over half a mile) and at 80 kilometers per hour (50 mph) it shoots you past the skyscrapers of Dubai, over the pristine blue marina dotted with mega yachts as off in the distance you see the serene expanse of the desert.

## Las Vegas

I also really loved ziplining down the middle of Fremont Street in old Las Vegas…you whizz past old school casinos, after being shot out of a slot machine! Seriously! The zipline is called Slotzilla, but even as someone who doesn't gamble, I don't mind getting up close and personal to this one!

## Mexico

I loved hanging upside down as I flew 300 feet in the air over the jungle on Puerto Vallarta's original zipline (the new one makes you lie down on your stomach in a sling). Both options are thrilling and potent!

And on my bucket list is paragliding…in Turkey.

## PARAGLIDE IN TURKEY

Oludeniz has one of the most beautiful beaches in Turkey, with pebble shores and a "blue lagoon" of aquamarine hues. The beach also happens to be one of the world's best places to paraglide, thanks to stable weather and gorgeous panoramic views. The launch site for most companies is from Babadağ mountain, with jumping-off points reaching 6,000 feet above sea level.

Okay that is pretty much straight out of the tour brochure, but it has sold me! I will be including this on my adventure travel tour to Turkey in 2025! Keep an eye on www.fionahorne.com for updates.

# PASSIONATE

## GLASS BOTTOM BRIDGES

One thing that could get you feeling the extreme element of Air is to walk across a 2073-foot-long glass bottom bridge spanning a verdant, ancient valley 500 feet below. The Bach Long is in Vietnam… recently built and the longest in the world. Bach Long means "White

Dragon" and the bridge's stark white tempered glass looks like the frozen breath of a mighty dragon.

China has 2,300 glass bottom bridges. The USA has 15, including the Grand Canyon Skywalk that juts out 70 feet from the edge of the canyon…and you look down 4,000 feet to the canyon floor! Japa, Canada, India, Australia…every country has glass bottomed bridges. Definitely a great way to take an "air bath."

## **WALKING OVER A SUSPENSION BRIDGE**

The only thing that could be more extreme than walking across a glass bottom bridge, is walking along a suspension bridge that's 721 meters long (2,365 feet) and 100 meters high (328 feet) and basically from a distance looks like a piece of rope strung between two mountains! Even I'm feeling my heart beat faster as I type this! So, this is definitely on my bucket list! But it earns its place in the Passionate tier because at the end of the day all you need to do is be able to walk across it.

The Sky Bridge 721 is the latest, longest suspension footbridge in the world. The previous holder of this record is the 516 Arouca bridge, in Portugal, which is "just" 516 meters in length (1,693 feet) and has an elevation of 175 meters (574 feet). It connects the banks of the Paiva River.

But at 721 meters long (almost half a mile), 95 meters high (312 feet), and just 1.2 meters wide (4 feet), this incredible feat of construction is in the Dolní Morava resort in East Bohemia, Czech Republic. It's in the foothills of the Jeseniky Mountains and straddles a valley with the Mlýnský stream in the distance below. Spanning two mountains, the Slaměnka and the Chlum, it's a spectacular feat of construction in an area of astonishing natural beauty. Okay, I lifted that from the tour brochure pretty much because I am completely green on the gifts of the Czech Republic. But not for long!

## KITE FLYING

Even though it is at the Passionate level, be aware that kite flying is still very adventuresome! Did you know there are aviation laws about flying kites?

For kite flying to be legal in Australia there are some very strict rules.

> **SPOKEN ON THE WIND**
>
> Wind-blown offerings, chanting, or singing in the wind are wonderful ways to align yourself with the element of Air before embarking on any extreme adventure.
>
> Go to a cliff or high building on a windy day. On a leaf, write your fears and with your left hand, throw it off the cliff/building so that it catches the breeze and floats away. On another leaf, write your best qualities with your right hand and throw it off the cliff so it catches the breeze and floats away.
>
> And then, chant your favorite mantra or sing your favorite song—whether it's Florence and the Machine, Taylor Swift, or AC/DC, go for it loud! Throw your arms in the air and raise energy as your breath flows in and out of you and spills out over the cliff/off the building as an offering to the Gods and Goddesses of the wind who can transform everything, vanquishing your fear and elevating your best qualities.

For example, the Australian Civil Aviation regulations state that you must not fly a kite more than 122 meters (400 feet) above ground level or within 4 kilometers (3 miles) of an airfield. You should avoid take-off and landing flight paths for aircraft.

As I pilot, I appreciate these rules a lot. Kites, along with drones (which also are operated under aviation laws), are definitely a problem should they appear in my flight path. Especially in critical phases of flight like take-offs and landings.

So, you may wonder if you can fly a kite in your backyard in the USA.

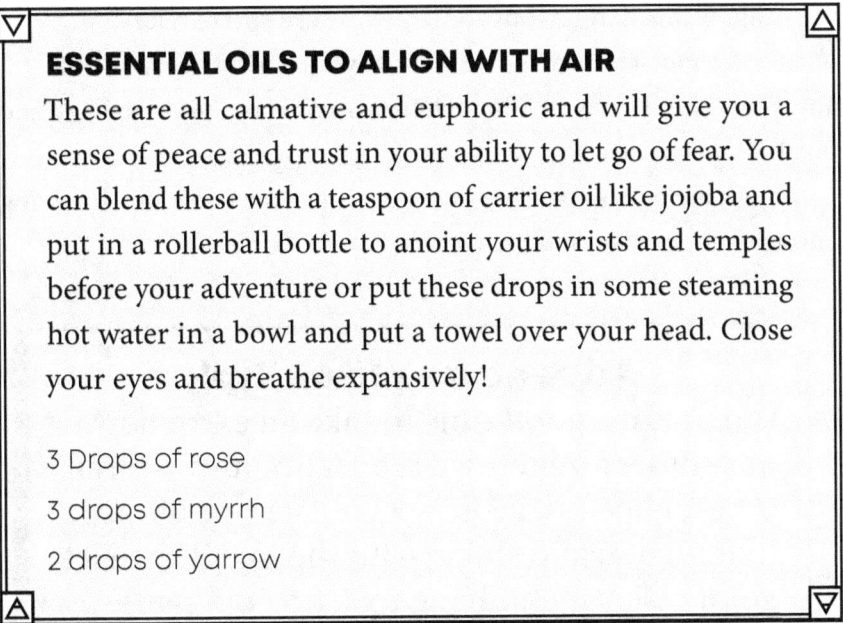

**ESSENTIAL OILS TO ALIGN WITH AIR**

These are all calmative and euphoric and will give you a sense of peace and trust in your ability to let go of fear. You can blend these with a teaspoon of carrier oil like jojoba and put in a rollerball bottle to anoint your wrists and temples before your adventure or put these drops in some steaming hot water in a bowl and put a towel over your head. Close your eyes and breathe expansively!

3 Drops of rose

3 drops of myrrh

2 drops of yarrow

According to the Federal Aviation Authority, no one may operate a kite more than 150 feet above the surface of the earth. This is usually suitable for general kite flying, and suitable for flying a kite in your backyard, so the answer is yes, but there are a lot more adventurous places you could go to fly kites.

When I lived in Old San Juan, Puerto Rico, I would watch the hundreds of kites flown every weekend by families on the large sweeping green hillslope that leads up to the 400+ year old El Morro Fort. All those years ago, medieval warriors fought their battles on this lawn and blood was spilt.

It is a beautiful affirmation of life and the value of it when you see parents and children launching kites together and flying them with huge smiles on their faces. But there is a downside to this happy spectacle. People's kite strings can break and kite strings and the litter of fallen kites become hazardous to the environment, getting looped around trees, plants, and bird life, and falling into the sea and creating hazards for the sea life. There are placards everywhere warning of this danger, but some people are still careless.

So be a conscious kite flyer and if your string breaks, collect it and your kite. Leave nothing where you flew but good energy and positive memories.

Kite flying is an expansive way to embrace the sweeping, inspiring, and transformative qualities of Air.

> **Adventure Witch Tip!**
> When is it a good time to take an extreme Air adventure? When we are feeling uninspired, bored, hopeless, depressed, isolated, pessimistic, judgmental and stuck, with the inability to let go of resentment, hang ups, and old patterns of thought, it's time to have an air bath!

## MOVIES ABOUT FLIGHT

Watching the two *Top Gun* movies puts you in the seat of flight—I absolutely love them along with aviation documentaries like *One Six Right: The Romance of Flying* (which includes the runway at Van Nuys on which I landed and passed my commercial check ride).

And any skydiving movie like the original *Point Break* (with Keanu Reeves and Patrick Swayze) which has the longest freefall known to anyone! It's totally not possible, but hey, it's Hollywood! And no, you can't talk to each other while you're in freefall! The scene when they all jump out of the plane is so crazy and funny, it doesn't make any sense to a real skydiver, but it's still awesome!

Or go and see the longest running ticketed film: *To Fly!*—showing for over 40 years at the Smithsonian. It's a half hour journey through the history of flight. The earth drops away beneath you as you ascend into the sky in an 1800's hot air balloon; you soar across the Arizona skies with the U.S. Navy's Blue Angels and blast off into space on a Saturn rocket.

Keep an eye on your local IMAX theater and make sure you go and see any movies they have about flight! Sitting back in a bucket chair, looking up at a giant screen surrounding you with a bird's eye view of the planet below will invoke the element of Air in a deeply satisfying way.

# ELEMENTAL INVOCATION: ISIS
## Worship and Invocation of the Great Goddess Isis

The Goddess Isis is the goddess of motherhood, magick, fertility, death, healing, and rebirth and also in ancient times revered as the Lady of the Living Air, Queen of the Winds, and Winged Goddess of the Spirit of Life. Her most ancient attributes established that from her we receive our breath and our life just as she fanned the breath of life into her brother/husband Osiris with her great and glorious wings, to bring him back to life. So, from her flows great magick of pure life-giving inspiration. Confidence, courage, and wisdom come when understanding the balance that arises from letting go and being reborn in her eyes. She is ultimately revered as the Great Mother who provides sustenance and who protects, in this world and the next.

> **THE BREATH OF LIFE**
> According to Ancient Egyptian mythology, Isis transformed herself into a bird to recover the pieces of her husband, Osiris's, body after it had been torn apart by his brother, Set. As she hovered over his reassembled corpse, she then used her great magick to bring him back to life. As such, the winged Isis is considered a powerful protective symbol.

Perform this ritual of worship to Isis and ask her to protect and inspire you as you embark on your extreme elemental air adventures.

**Blend the following in a teaspoon of carrier oil like jojoba or sweet almond:**

3 drops frankincense

3 drops myrrh

2 drops rose or blue lotus

Light a white candle in honor of Isis—there are many colors and attributes associated with her, and white can encompass them all.

Meditate on the flame and turn your attention to your fears.

Think about your Air adventure and observe where you feel fear or concern. Where does that live in your body? When you can identify where it is, anoint that part of your body. For example, you may feel fear in your feet when considering jumping out of an airplane—so anoint the soles of your feet with this oil.

When you are anointed where you feel guided to, place your hands over your heart and take seven deep breaths—feel your chest rise and fall as the air around you moves in and out of your lungs.

Temple of Philae, sacred to Isis, Egypt

Be blessed as Isis fans her wings of great magick upon you and chant the following seven times with reverence.

*Glory to you Goddess*
*Great Mother Isis,*
*May I be protected in this life*
*By your blessed Magick.*
*May your sacred wings hold me*
*As I awaken to the joy at the core of your creation*
*Glory to you Goddess.*
*Great Mother, Isis.*

Snuff the candle and relight and take seven deep breaths when you need to feel held and protected.

Remember to breathe as you embark on your adventure and every time you consciously do, know that Isis's wings are fanning that air into your lungs, availing you of her invigoration and protection.

# EARTH

When we think of Earth, we think of being anchored to the present moment and embracing the presence of what is. In my spellcasting, I have always relied on the element of Earth to draw my visualizations and projections to manifest in the physical plane. When Earth energy is in balance, you feel fulfilled, connected to the meaning of life and your purpose. It lays the foundation upon which the other elements can be expressed and experienced. In balance we feel free… to care for and support ourselves and others without becoming drained or exhausted.

## TRANSCENDENT

### MEDITATION WITHIN THE KING'S CHAMBER

When I first saw the Great Pyramid of Giza, across a stretch of dirt as I whizzed along a highway in a van, and then shortly after from the balcony of my hotel room, I did not think it could possibly be a tomb. It struck me more as a machine, the precision of its outside walls was just too perfect. I had a moment where I saw water lapping at its edges in a vision. I wondered if somehow the water would enter the pyramid under pressure and create an electrical charge.

And then, when I entered the pyramid, its steep geometric corridors and square cuts into the walls echoed even more of the workings of a machine…not a tomb for a dead pharaoh.

Earlier that same day I had been trawling underground in the

Valley of the Kings, the elaborate hieroglyphics and carvings telling the story of the dead more than these stark bare walls with strange scorch marks on them!

Ascending into the King's Chamber of the Great Pyramid

I entered the King's Chamber late at night—though it could have been any time of the day as it was black as black in there except for a thin fluorescent tube that ran around the edges of the space.

I felt a sense of peace and solitude, despite the fact that I was with a group of 20 others who were murmuring and complaining of feeling hot and claustrophobic. The distractions could not take away from me a feeling that bordered on suspended animation and yet, at the same time, an electrical excitement that coursed through my body. I did not feel hot. I did not feel smothered…I felt electrically alive!

Having a private experience in this room in the center of the pyramid, surrounded by hundreds of thousands of tons of rock and earth while the geometrically precise structure around you with its secret corridors and rooms jets up into the sky in a dramatic mechanical way, feels surprisingly organic. It felt like plugging into Mother Earth—the Great Pyramid bristles with her power and energy.

After having some time in the King's Chamber, I descended to the Queen's Chamber below. It is a smaller room and has unusual cutouts in the wall, including small square holes about five feet from the floor and just wide enough to stick your arms through.

I asked a guard that was there what were those strange square holes? And he spoke excellent English and told me that in 2019 scientists had come and put cameras on wires into the holes…and they were actually shafts that went along for 30 meters (98 feet) before coming to a small wooden door with copper handles. The scientists drilled holes in the doors and put the cameras through… and the holes continue for another 30 meters, where they came to another small wooden door with copper handles.

I asked him what was the conclusion as to why these shafts and doors existed and he said that "Cheops had them designed so that his spirit could ascend in stages and secretly leave the pyramid and come back without being seen." I found that fascinating, and also completely implausible. What is the most efficient conductor of electricity? Copper! Could those shafts not be part of the design of a power plant?

Would you like to see these shafts and form your own opinion?

I will be excited to offer this private experience of the King's Chamber as part of my spiritual adventures to Egypt that I will be leading from 2024. In addition to exploring the accessible inner chambers of the Great Pyramid, there will be a silent ceremony and an opportunity to feel into the space that is one of the most dense and quiet you could ever experience going up, instead of going under.

## SURVIVOR

Why would I put my experiences on 2006's *Australian Celebrity Survivor* in the Earth section? Because it was the ultimate crash course in survival of the earth—as in planet earth.

As we were set upon separate beaches by boat, us contestants were truly given nothing to support our survival. We were initially split into gender specific tribes and told that the creek had clean water (which was changed to being where all the plastic water bottles were placed when the producers realized drinking from the creek would give us giardia). That first evening, as the sun set and we had barely any shelter from looming storm clouds overhead and the sand was starting to move as millions of tiny hermit crabs started getting busy for the evening, I started looking at things differently. Giant banana leaves became roofing material; a tree became not only a source of building materials, but cutlery for eating dinner, and piles of its pine needles a soft mattress to sleep on.

Survival became a holistic experience of making shelter, finding food and water, and (if I wasn't taking part in a cutthroat competitive reality TV series) peace and reflection. I lasted a week, which equated to two episodes, before being voted off by a double-crossing fellow tribe member who was voted off the following week by the people who convinced her to vote me off.

A giant banana leaf also became a beach towel, and one of the happiest memories of my life is lying alone upon it one night on the deserted beach on the edge of a tiny island in the vast Pacific Ocean… the stars so bright in the sky I felt I could reach out my hand and pluck them like cherries. A year later I wrote a song called "Lost in The Woods" about the experience for my solo album, *Witchweb* (you can hear it by visiting my website www.fionahorne.com).

*The stars, so close like cherries*
*Ripe in the sky*
*I let their sweet light*
*Blind my urban eyes*
*For good*
*Lost in the woods*

To have your own deep Earth immersion experience, there are weekend survival and wilderness courses abundantly available now given the popularity of reality survival shows.

Here is an example of what is offered at a course. Adventure Out is a company that specializes in Earth survival skills. They are based in California, which is where I am currently writing this book, and their courses give a great idea of what you can learn when you strip away all the padding and truly set your feet on the bare earth.

They call themselves an "epicenter for primitive skills and wilderness survival instruction." I love the way they offer an immersive raw experience of the land, in a very populated and modern tech laden area (Silicone Valley anyone?).

They find areas which still have original California landscape and teach skills of shelter, water, fire and food. This includes animal tracking, stone tools and lots more. I baulk at the animal hunting part, being vegetarian. But I also respect the role that this kind of survival and associated life skills have played with the original custodians and how people choose to live their lives using only what they need to survive, with respect and reverence for the land and life.

When I went to Alaska in the depths of a sunless, almost 24 hours-a-day winter with my friend, who is an Alaskan native and did outreach work with the Inuit, we visited a local family and I was offered moose when we shared a meal. I ate a small portion with respect. Hunting the moose is a rite of passage that a youth coming into maturity performs, and that one moose feeds the family for the entire winter, and often the village too.

Learning survival skills is not just a physical endeavor but a spiritual one too.

## HIKE THE WORLD'S MOST DANGEROUS HIKING TRAIL

My girlfriend, travel photographer and documentary film maker Amy Vankanan, hiked to Mt. Everest base camp and she is a powerhouse of hiking! She has hiked the mountains of Pakistan and visited remote tribes there. She has asked me to join her on a number of occasions. But I have to have a reality check. Jumping around on stage for decades, teaching spin classes for years, and recently pushing heavy baggage carts across bumpy airport access ramps that jarred every joint in my body (being a pilot of the Caribbean is not the glamor job some would think it is!) means I am not going to commit to a multi-day-long extreme hike and potentially hold up my companions. That being said, the photos she took and the stories she told me, make this truly one of those ultimate bucket list items in the Transcendent category…and that is "just" getting to base camp. (See for yourself at her Instagram: @amyvankanan)

Right now, this adventure below is more up my bucket list alley because you can do it in a day!

Rivalling Everest for the most demanding hike and officially called "the most dangerous hike in the world" is Mt. Huashan in

China. You can find this mountain near the city of Huayin in the area where the famous Terracotta Warriors were found. The region is considered the 3000-year-old cradle of Chinese culture.

After a network of dangerous and precipitous trekking trails allows you to access the Huashan mountain's five summits, there is a solitary building of worship or a "tea house" on the southern face of each of the five summits at over 7,000 feet high. And you can even play chess in the beautiful traditional structures there, if you have time before having to get back down before evening fog and weather sets in. The five points of the "summits" form the points of a lotus flower—a revered symbol of enlightenment and openness.

But the hikes up sheer cliff faces to reach these lofty heights, nicknamed in English "The Plank Walk", have a rumored 100 fatalities a year. Other names for the most challenging trails include: Thousand-Foot Precipice, Hundred-Foot Crevice, and Black Dragon Ridge.

But these incredible, extreme hikes lead to a steaming pot of tea made with rainwater or snowmelt and mountain springs at a Taoist temple found atop the west peak called Cuiyun Palace.

Since getting sober 11 years ago, I have become a tea aficionado! I savor teas for their subtle scents and layers of flavors, the way I used to love the ritual of smelling and sipping red wine. So, I will be very happy to climb a treacherous trail to sit and sip tea!

Taoism is China's indigenous spirituality, which arose in the 4th century B.C. and in the 2nd century B.C. a Taoist temple was established at the base of Mount Huashan. Since that time pilgrims, monks, and nuns have lived on the mountain and in the surrounding area to maintain the deep reverence for the region even as adventure tourists now swarm the area.

"Tao," which translates as "the path" or "the way" of the Universe, emphasizes that humans must aspire to live in a state of harmony with all things. This concept is honored by the meditative process of walking the paths and scaling the five peaks, as they lead to tea on Mt. Huashan. Laozi, the author of the *Tao Te Ching*, was said to have been served the first cup of ceremonial tea as part of the first Taoist observance.

The fact that there is a teahouse building on each peak and one still serving tea to those who scale the heights is a testament to the spiritual and religious significance of this enormous epicenter of powerful Earth elemental energy. In Taoism the element of Earth is considered the grounding peacekeeper that nourishes us and anchors us in the present moment.

It is beautiful that the most difficult and challenging paths on this mountain symbolically lead to one of the most sacred forms of enlightenment and inner peace, called "Yang Sheng" in Taoist philosophy.

> "Taoism seeks to organize the body and mind to 'nurture life,' an art called 'Yang Sheng.' It means to adjust your lifestyle habits, such as meditation, physical environment, the food you eat, exercise habits—how you can create a holistic system for well-being and through these habits, one becomes aligned with nature, and those who are deeply in touch with themselves will naturally express ethics and morality. Meditation is vital to reach this state, and tea is at the center of it. Drinking it with a quiet mind and awareness allows the senses to open—to stop, look and listen."
>
> —Ken Cohen, 62, a Taoist scholar and tea master, world renowned health educator and Qigong Grand Master. Author of *The Way of Qigong: The Art and Science of Energy Healing* (Random House, 1999)

# POTENT

## DUNES

In 2016 I took myself on a flying safari of Namibia. While this was an ultimate Air adventure, it also embraced deep connection with the ancient Earth on this part of the planet.

In addition to exploring the intriguing spiral scarred rocks of 1,500-feet-deep, 500-million-year-old Fish River Canyon, I climbed barefoot to the top of the luscious red dome of the largest sand dune in the oldest desert in the world. This dune is near Sossusvlei and is nicknamed Big Daddy at 325 meters high (1,066 feet).

Exploring Deadvlei, Namib-Naukluft Park, Namibia

It was soothing to watch my feet sink into the warm red sand that glistened with tiny crystal particles as I made my way to the top.

There are only two colors up there—the red sand below and the blue sky above. I sensed my crown chakra open as my sacral shot down into the earth. And I was suspended energetically in a beautifully anchoring and invigorating way.

> **EARTH**
>
> There are two words that describe a sense of being out of Earth balance: worried and needy. And these feelings and perceptions of reality spin off into obsessive fearful behavior, scattered thinking, clingy and insecure behavior, and a lack of positive routine. The unbalance can even manifest as the opposite: being overly obsessive as you try to create a sense of "control" on the shifting sands of life.
>
> As a nomad, I know I can start to feel overly emotional. When I am feeling low and exhausted or spread thin and scattered, I describe myself as a piece of driftwood, floating on the surface of the ocean and banging up against any shore without purpose or direction.
>
> When I start thinking like this, it's time to balance my Earth energy! Even just lying on the bare earth can help. Pushing my hands through mud or clay can help. (Pottery classes! There's a thought!)
>
> One of the things I love doing best when I am out of Earth balance is making a salt hand scrub and slowly massaging my hands and wrists with it, morning and night—I express myself a lot through my hands and I find this intensely soothing and grounding when I am losing the plot.

Later that day I explored the nearby Deadvlei, a stark white clay pan, surrounded by vibrant red dunes and studded with 900-year-old dead camel thorn trees. So beautiful in their black, stark preservation.

The takeaway from this is to find a sand dune somewhere near you—or plan the trip of a lifetime to Namibia—and make sure you climb it in bare feet to deeply align with the grounding Earth energy that also honors the one constant in life: change. Just like the sand dunes are constantly shifting and changing, so are our lives.

## THE CRYSTAL MOUNTAIN IN THE WESTERN DESERT

On my bucket list and soon to be experienced at the time of writing this, is the Crystal Mountain on the edge of the White Desert, in the Western Desert region of Egypt.

Extreme elemental Earth alignment can be experienced here when exploring an exhumed cave, complete with stalagmites and stalactites that have been thrust upwards by Earth movement. With time, the cave has lost its roof to erosion and has almost weathered away. The crystal in "Crystal Mountain" is calcite that formed in the paleolithic caves of Khoman Chalk in the Western Desert.

Magickally, Calcite is considered to offer strength of spirit and energy, while being a stone of amplification. As you wander amongst the studded hexagonal stalks jutting out of the desert floor, I'm sure it is truly invigorating and grounding…I can't wait to find out for myself!

## ROAD TRIP TO VEGAS

Well maybe a bit further past Vegas—the Valley of Fire is just 58 miles from the Strip, in the Mojave Desert, and where one of my favorite road trip memories lies.

I had taken my fire dancing *poi* and some fuel as I wanted to light up as the sun set against the vast red rocks. It was winter and there was no fire ban. The Valley of Fire consists of bright red sandstone outcrops hugged by gray and tan limestone mountains. The sandstone is from the Jurassic period and is the remnant of the sand left behind by the wind after inland seas subsided and the land rose. Early humans moved into southern Nevada as far back as 11,000 years ago. The most obvious evidence of occupation is the petroglyphs carved into the rocks by the Basketmaker culture about 2,500 years ago, followed later by the Early Pueblo culture.

There is a deep silence there and I lay on the warm rocks to soak in the Earth energy before lighting up and firedancing.

The Valley of Fire was used as a film set for the blockbuster movie *The Martian*. In fact, I went and saw it at the cinema the day before actually going there in person—but you don't even need to have this prompt to feel like you are in another part of the solar system when a setting sun ignites everything into an even richer, redder glow.

Road trips in the USA (because of the great condition of the roads as opposed to somewhere like Egypt!) are a great way to connect with extreme Earth energy. The act of moving across the ground and immersing yourself in adventures along the way anchors you in the present moment in a positively proactive way. Creating an itinerary that embraces all five elements is an option, or focus on national parks like the Mighty Five in Utah (only a couple of hours away from the Valley of Fire) that include Zion, Bryce Canyon, Capitol Reef, Arches, and Canyonlands. The Mars-like landscapes continue to evolve here, inviting an ever-expanding sense of awe and wonder at the magnificence of these rocks tumbling around us in space and upon which we live.

## WILDERNESS IMMERSION

In the Transcendent section above, I suggest doing a survival course, but there is another approach to aligning with Earth energy and that is wilderness immersion. This can be forest bathing in Japan amongst native Japanese conifers such as *sugi* or *hinoki*; walking amongst the giant Sequoia trees in Muir Woods, Northern California; or strolling amongst towering gum trees in Australia. The positive grounding (read aligning with Earth energy) effects of forest bathing can be felt by walking in any natural environment and consciously connecting with the earth. Bare feet first!

> **WHAT IS FOREST BATHING?**
>
> The term emerged in Japan in the 1980's as a physiological and psychological exercise called *shinrin-yoku* ("forest bathing" or "taking in the forest atmosphere"). Japanese cities were one of the most tech-burned out, high stress environments on the planet, and forest bathing was encouraged to help combat this and also to inspire the city's residents to reconnect with and protect the country's forests.
>
> Japan created the term *shinrin-yoku*, but the healing concept of merging with nature has been expounded by many cultures. The natural world is good for human health. It seems so obvious to a Witch who reveres nature as sacred. But we often need to be reminded of this in our tech-heavy lives.

There is a company in Malibu that offers courses in wilderness immersion. Their mission statement states that they offer fun and therapeutic programs that connect people to nature, enhance quality of life, and assist in developing personal power to create capable individuals. Their courses include: earthing, Qigong, nature yoga, fox walking (I wonder what this is?!) energy medicine, stone balancing, nature listening, the Zen of archery, interpretative nature hikes, natural movement exercises, animal tracking and observation, tree climbing and sky swinging, Native American skills, crafts and lore, and integrated quiet meditative time. I love that all these processes are offered in a weekend course environment. Simple, potent steps to earth yourself in a magickal adventurous life. Every skill and experience shines a light on the next one. Who knows where you may be drawn to as you explore these skills that will resonate so deeply in your primal matrix?

## BUCKET LIST: UNDERGROUND AT GÖBEKLI TEPE

Almost 12,000 years old, this monumental underground temple in Turkey dates to a time considered to be pre-civilization. The very existence of Göbekli Tepe has forced archaeologists to re-think the dawn of civilization. This Neolithic collection of stone circles is the oldest temple currently discovered ever built by mankind—it eclipses the Pyramids at Giza by nearly 7,000 years.

Over twenty sites make up the entire complex and it defies comprehension. For a start, it is 6,000 years older than Stonehenge! To put this in perspective, there is as much time between the construction of Göbekli Tepe and the construction of Stonehenge as there is between the construction of Stonehenge and today! Elaborate artwork and carvings decorate it…6,000 years before writing was invented.

It was built right around the same time that the last ice age ended and the people who built it went on to be an active civilization for nearly three millennia before the temple was abandoned under mysterious circumstances. The fact that much of the site was backfilled before being abandoned seeds a huge mystery—who built this place of worship? Who lived here and who tried to erase evidence that it ever existed?

The craftsmanship on display is thousands of years ahead of its time. The feat of engineering, project management, and the manpower to build it should be impossible based on assumptions of ancient civilizations. Thinking of Neolithic humans carving the elaborate images with stone age tools seems…unfeasible!

This barely lifts the lid on the marvels of Göbekli Tepe and it is my dream to walk the raised wooden walkways around the site and spend an entire day there. It is off the main tourist track of Turkey, in the region of East Anatolia which is modern day southeast Turkey. It is located on the northern edge of The Fertile Crescent, which is where the dawn of civilization occurred, an area where humans were able to live off the rich and bountiful land that stretched between the Tigris and Euphrates rivers across modern day Syria, Turkey, and northern Iraq.

I am adding this region to my nourishing spiritual adventure tours in 2025—if you want to travel with me, join my Patreon for the first chance to book and special discounts: www.patreon.com/fionahorne.

## PASSIONATE

### READ

Read *Underland* by Robert MacFarlane, a thrilling and enchanting book about places underground, including rivers under Patagonia, catacombs under Paris, and uranium mines under Mexico.

You are taken on a journey through caves, caverns, underground rivers, and the labyrinths of mythology, some so remote and extraordinary in physical reality that it makes the earthen core of our planet a place of mystery and fantasy. When it in reality, like the element of Earth, it anchors us to our humanity. Some of the experiences underground are forged by nature and others by human interaction and they all weave the thread of our experiential interpretation as to how the "lands" affect us—even "just" reading about them.

### CAVES ROAD SOUTHWEST AUSTRALIA

I spent the COVID years living in Western Australia, not far from a 100-kilometer-long ribbon of tar called Caves Road. A chain of 150 limestone caves stretches along the road. Four are open to the public and are beautifully set up and curated for deeply satisfying human exploration.

Descending deep into the labyrinth of structures in the various caves makes you feel like you are experiencing the planet by being welcomed into various homes of the Gods of the First Nation indigenous Australians. Ngilgi Cave was not far from where I lived, and one of the most frequented caves by tourists...and it has an elaborate Dreamtime story:

> *Ngilgi Cave is named after one of the Wardandi Aboriginal people's 'Dreamtime' spirits. Ngilgi was a good spirit who lived in the ocean, while Wolgine was a bad spirit who once lived in the cave.*

> *"A long time ago, the entrance to the cave was near the ocean, where the little brook comes out. Food was plenty, and the Aboriginal people used to collect their water from the entrance to the cave. Then an evil spirit called Wolgine began lurking in the cave. Wolgine caused the water hole to dry up and food to become scarce. He drew unwary people into the great hole of darkness—never to be seen again. Ngilgi, who always watched over the tribes in the area, saw the suffering of his people, and decided to do something about Wolgine. He spoke with other good spirits of the ocean and together they planned to rid the district of the evil spirit Wolgine. So, the spirits of the waves, the wind, the rain, thunder, and lightning joined together and made the most terrifying*

*storm. The ocean formed itself into huge waves and the wind pushed them up into the entrance of the cave. A fierce battle followed—Wolgine was driven further and further into the cave with the sea following him. Finally, driven to the end of the cave, he knew he was beaten and begged for mercy. Ngilgi told Wolgine he could go, providing he never came back to the area again. So Wolgine burst out of the cave; creating the entrance as we know it today, -and ran away as fast as he could—never to be seen again. With Wolgine gone forever, the food once again became plentiful and Ngilgi claimed the cave as his home. From that day on it became known as 'Ngilgi's nurilem mia' (Ngilgi's cave house)."*

—From Capes Foundation: "History and Aboriginal Culture"

www.capesfoundation.org.au

My favorite is Jewel Cave—it's 1.9 kilometers long (1.2 miles) and exists under a forest of giant karri trees whose leaves whisper "hush" as you descend through an iron door and down steep stairs into an enormous cathedral-like chamber, softly lit by artful human effort. There are three huge caverns and a spectacular straw stalactite—one of the longest in the world at five meters (16.4 feet). In 1960, the fossil of the now extinct Tasmanian Tiger was found there—opening a mystery of how this animal got here—and other unusual fossils in found in the cave. Did they fall into the cave? Or is there another reason?

Jewel Cave, Southwest Australia
(Photo by Author)

## **TV BINGE ON SURVIVAL REALITY SHOWS**

Watch *Alone* on TV, and any other survival shows about individuals living close to the earth. Try and find ones that are sincere and not an exercise in group drama (like the one I was on)!

## EARTHING HAND SCRUB

You will need:

1/3 cup shea butter

½ cup fine cane sugar

½ cup of semi-coarse sea salt (a little coarser than the sugar)

½ cup quality virgin olive oil

10 drops lavender oil

8 drops chamomile oil

½ cup of semi-coarse sea salt (a little coarser than the sugar)

Whip the shea butter and oil together first and then slowly add the sugar and salt, gently stirring. Finally, add the essential oils and stir through. Put in a glass jar with a lid and keep by the sink where you will have it easily on hand when you need to feel grounded. I find massaging this into dry hands works best and then rinse off after with warm water and pat dry gently. The salt draws out nervous energy and excess tension, the lavender and chamomile are soothing, and the oil and shea butter will keep moisturizing your hands for hours after.

Earth as an elemental energy is not only about rocks and dirt and crystals! I experience a deep elemental exchange by stepping out of modern technological conveniences and getting in touch with our raw primal sense of being. Watching some of the true reality survival shows can really trigger the Earth dwelling reflex, which may seem contradictory. But when you are stuck inside or recuperating from other extreme adventures, it's an effective way to learn and get inspired for your next adventure!

> **ESSENTIAL OILS TO ALIGN WITH EARTH**
>
> Frankincense
>
> Spruce
>
> Pine
>
> Juniper
>
> Rosewood
>
> Geranium
>
> Use one or a blend of these (combine a drop or two of up to three oils in a teaspoon of carrier oil like jojoba, coconut, or olive) and massage into the base of your neck and soles of your feet before you walk or lie on bare earth. It will ground you with a sense of "can do" and integrative physical/mental confidence before you embark on an extreme Earth adventure.

## GARDENING

A passionate level of interaction that can stimulate a deep resonance with the earth is gardening. The cycles of life, death, and rebirth will play out in the life of your garden. As you see those cycles reflected in your life, maybe they will reveal a side of life you have never experienced before. Consider writing self-limiting beliefs and fears on pieces of organic paper in natural ink and placing the paper as compost under your plants and allowing that energy to be recycled into positive personal growth and rebirth, fueling your desire for more extreme magickal adventures!

# ELEMENTAL INVOCATION: GAIA
## Worship and Invocation of the Great Mother, Gaia

My first patron Goddess before Lilith (who became the patron Goddess of my first coven) was the ancient Greek Goddess Gaia. Early in my Witch life, from a little esoteric store, I bought the original green seated Millennial Gaia statue forged by Oberon and Morning Glory Zell. At the time, all things pagan and witchy were extremely rare and this potent creation stoked a fire of fascination and reverence in me for the Great Mother that has anchored my Witchcraft all these years.

In the extreme elemental adventures, I suggest bonding with Earth in its planetary essence is key, and so worshipping this ancient Greek Goddess who has become synonymous with pagan and Witchcraft practices is aligned.

Create a shrine to Gaia in earthy colors and contents. I have kept rocks and dirt from all the sacred sites I have visited, and I place these on my altar to her along with quartz and obsidian crystal.

The snake and its shedding skin is sacred to Gaia, and I have collected snakeskin since my first snake familiar Lulu and more recently when bushwalking in the Australian outback. I always include that on my Gaia altar if I can.

A wooden image or statue of Gaia is a great way to connect with her. If you don't have a specific image, choose something that resonates with you. It may be a picture of the earth, or a particular stone or crystal. If you don't know, close your eyes and ask her what to use…and use the first thing that comes to you as appropriate.

A bowl of water with a pinch of sea salt can represent her vast oceans. In the all-embracing elemental essence of Earth, having Water, incense (Air), and a candle (Fire) all serve to venerate the Great Mother.

Every day leading up to your extreme Earth adventure, make an offering at your shrine to Gaia. Traditionally, in ancient times, she was offered honey, barley, and water.

I also suggest the following:

Hold a special crystal of your choice to your heart and empower it with the following devotion by speaking it out aloud so that your voice and heartbeat vibrate though the crystal.

*Great Mother*
*I honor thee, source of all life,*
*May you keep me safe,*
*So that I may always know and worship you*
*In this realm and the next*

Place the crystal back on the altar and meditate for a few minutes at the altar, paying attention to any messages, feelings, or signs that may come to you. Take action on these if indicated.

Carry the crystal with you when you embark on your extreme Earth adventure!

# SPIRIT

Integrating the fifth element of Spirit into our lives comes down to one very simple truth, which I will share from my perspective.

All the different components and events of my life, the people, places and things, the feelings, physical and emotional, spiritual, and extraterrestrial on every level have one thing very specific thing in common…ME! And my perspective of them.

And that is the way to understand how to align with the fifth element, Spirit.

It is YOU. It is ME.

And it is the most magickal of them all.

When Spirit is out of balance, we feel lost in a sea of indecision and self-doubt. We feel cut off from a sense of awe and wonder in the world. We feel that we have no purpose and no meaning. We feel unconnected.

When the Spirit element is aligned, we feel purposeful and peaceful; we feel we have everything we need; we feel we are enough.

We feel connected.

## TRANSCENDENT

### DARK RETREATS

I was the host of the TV reality show *Mad Mad House* for Syfy Channel. In the show, ten "everyday world" contestants competed to gain the favor of the "Alts" which included me, the Witch, a naturist, a Voodoo priestess, a modern primitive, and a vampire. One of the challenges I created for the guests was to sit in a structure in complete darkness for eight hours to contemplate the meaning of their existence. The guests were blindfolded, and the structure was low and made of woven branches. They had to sit on a folded rug, cross-legged. The girl that completed the challenge (Jamie—who went on to win the grand prize of $100,000) said it was a profoundly enriching experience for her. At first very confronting but ultimately liberating. If just eight hours can do that, imagine what eight days would be like! Or maybe just to start, three or five days.

Fiona Horne Promo from SyFy's Mad, Mad House (2004)

In Southern Oregon on 100,000 acres of property are two Hobbit-like dugout structures and a straw bale rolled house. The place is called Sky Cave, and it is the home of dark retreats.

A dark retreat sees you enter into a small space, 300 square feet (smaller than the Great Pyramid's King's Chamber) and after a period of integration you sleep, stand, take a bath, lie down on the floor, in total darkness and total silence for anywhere from three to five days or longer.

This is on my bucket list of things to do. Even though I will never experience silence again with my crazy loud relentless tinnitus (ringing in my ears from exposure to loud music during my years touring the world in Def FX and too much head banging!) I would love to experience and learn with this cocooning against the sharp edges of reality.

The idea of complete sensory deprivation underground feels like heaven. Heaven born of Mother Earth—maybe that's why they call it "Sky Cave."

People who emerge after their period of darkness say that it is like being reborn. While you are alone in the dark, you have the opportunity to understand and journey through the expanse of what lies within you. It is the ultimate immersion into the Spirit element.

The couple who own Sky Cave have been running dark retreats since 2019, wishing to offer a healing modality that is rare in the western world but more common in other cultures and has a vast, ancient heritage.

Retreating into total darkness has been a practice for many of the ancient spiritual traditions from around the world. Dark rooms have appeared in many different forms—from the pyramids for the ancient Egyptians, to the catacombs for the ancient Romans, the cells of the 15th century French mystics, and the caves for the Kogi Mamos in Colombia, along with the lamas, monks, adepts and sincere practitioners throughout India, Tibet, China, and other parts of the world.

In total darkness, the vast magnificence of the world within awakens.

Dzogchen practitioners (from the Tibetan traditions of Buddhism) spend years in preliminary and regenerative stage practices before even entering into dark retreat. This also holds true for many ancient and traditional Taoist and Hindu practitioners.

The Kogi Mamos of Colombia are highly respected tribal priests and are taken from birth and put in a cave for the first nine years of their lives to undergo strict training and discipline to assume this role. Elder Mamos, along with their birth mother, care for, train, and teach the child.

In India, dark retreat is often coupled with Kaya Kalpa retreats for very advanced practitioners. Kaya Kalpa is a specialized field highly revered within the Ayurveda and Siddha medical systems for regenerating the body. It is traditionally done alone in darkness along with the application of various herbal concoctions.

---

**FROM SKY CAVE'S WEBSITE:**

"Benefits and Blessings

"MOVING BEYOND ALL CULTURAL & SPIRITUAL OVERLAYS - SIMPLY RESTING INTO THAT WHICH REMAINS.

"When we enter into the darkness - we see our confusion more clearly - and we slowly begin to feel what matters most. We touch a profound freedom as we simply soften into the vast timeless space that enfolds us.

"The darkness invites us into a core-splitting honesty where we are moved beyond our constant posturing.

"As we let go of our ongoing attempts to control our world, and even our subtle ways of controlling our inner-world, we begin to simply rest exactly as we are."

---

You can contact Sky Cave Retreats by visiting their website www.skycaveretreats.com. Once settled in, you get two organic meals a day sourced from produce grown on the farm, served to you once a day through a double door. There is a hot bath to enjoy inside your retreat, a comfy bed, and total darkness and silence for three to five days…or more.

As I was researching more about dark retreats for westerners, they can be found in diverse environments from Guatemala to New York.

An Englishman who spent three weeks over Christmas in a dark retreat in Mexico describes the experience as deeply healing and restorative…and also at times hallucinogenic. When we don't eat for some time, the body eventually feeds on itself, clearing out junk from the cells in a healthy process called "autophagy." In the same way, when the mind has nothing to feed on, a kind of mental autophagy occurs as the mind processes what has been long locked away in the subconscious.

This phenomenon is catalyzed by DMT, a psychedelic compound produced in small amounts after around four days in the dark. Uniquely among psychedelics, DMT is produced naturally by the body—in particular at birth and death, which is why many with near-death experiences report experiences indistinguishable from DMT trips.

On a dark retreat, there is a lot of time to process stored memories, trauma, and to unlearn emotional attachments to things. There is time to reveal the true nature of Spirit, the element that weaves it all together in your life.

## VIPASSANA

A long time ago when I was in my 90's band, Def FX, which was a very successful charting and touring band, my life was punctuated with extremely loud concerts, frantic travel all over the country, different hotels, sometimes six flights in a week, sometimes 18 hours of driving across the country in a van crammed with the other band members, or being in a recording studio for hours and hours. My life was an explosion of noise, pressure, adrenaline and excitement, and exhaustion and depression, as I struggled to weave the experiences together in a meaningful way that was anchored in self-worth. I dealt with terrible insecurity that somehow, I was not good enough or worthy of this attention.

Vipassana meditation in the Eastern Desert, Egypt

In my 20s it was a crisis of self-identity and ego, which is normal for any growing human, but it was supercharged by the extraordinary circumstances I was in.

During this time, I was increasingly drawn to alternative spirituality. It was where my Witchcraft really took root, as I carved out small moments of time to practice some ritual and explore concepts of spell casting. Strangely enough, this is how I discovered Vipassana. I wanted to be able to focus unwaveringly on one thing, to raise power to fuel my intention towards a spell coming to fruition in a way that I determined was appropriate and expected. I was still learning that sometimes the outcome of spells is not what you think you want; it's what the universe knows you need! But I digress!

I saw a small, printed pamphlet about Vipassana in an esoteric bookstore in Sydney Australia. Despite the grueling touring schedule of the band, I realized there was a 10-day Vipassana course being offered in the Blue Mountains, 100 kilometers west of Sydney that I could attend.

I went straight from the Sydney TV studio of channel 9, where I was interviewed for the show *60 minutes*, about tinnitus, to the retreat, arriving in the late afternoon.

After the noise of the city and all the attention in the TV studio, I was struck by the immense peace, the simple buildings dotted amongst the giant blue eucalyptus tree forest on the ridge of a mountain.

Over the course of the next days, I entered a vow of silence. I did not look anyone else in the eyes. I meditated in a sitting position for 14 hours a day and ate simple vegetarian meals twice a day.

Every morning before sunrise, a monk would walk through the grounds sounding a gong. I and the three other girls I shared I room with would silently get up from our single bunk beds, wrap ourselves in warm blankets, and walk in single procession to the meditation hall. Women on one side, men on the other. There were over 100 of us. At the front of the hall was a teacher sitting in lotus position. I sat in lotus position on a small wooden block, folding my legs underneath me and arranging my blankets around me. The teacher pressed play on a cassette deck and the voice of S.N. Goenka, the teacher of Vipassana "insight meditation" who brought it to the West out of Burma, would speak. His deep mellifluous tones would coax me into a peaceful place of observing the area above my upper lip where the air leaving my nostrils flowed, forwards and backwards, in and out.

For the first three days, 14 hours a day, that's all we did. This is called learning the practice of *anapana*. The world of my upper lip became the edges of the universe to me, every hair follicle was a tree and my breath swelled amongst the trunks and branches, all of them. Microscopic creatures dotted the terrain. Even when I was eating in the hall with the others, all silently and all with our eyes lowered and observing Grand Silence, I was focused on the forest perched on my upper lip.

On the morning of the 4th day, the teacher put a different tape in the player and S.N. Goenka taught us to take that awareness and sweep it through our entire body. This is where we learned Vipassana.

It was the most blissful and extraordinary experience of my life at the time, eclipsing any of the euphoria I experienced on stage with thousands of people in the audience. It eclipsed the most expensive glass of champagne, or any other worldly prop of existence. It was so blissful and I was so acutely aware of life, Spirit, and the divinity of it all, that my original goal of being able to focus on one thing to enhance my spellcasting was forgotten.

Vipassana is actually not about concentrating on one thing—it's about the cultivation and experience of mindfulness and equanimity.

When we left the hall after receiving the Vipassana instruction, I went for a walk in the gardens. I remember climbing a tree to the very top of its leafy canopy with no effort. I was vibrating and at one with all things. I bounded up that tree like I was a monkey quickly easily and effortlessly. I sat in the branches looking out across the tops of the mountains and just felt like everything made sense. I made sense, and I was free.

Six days later, after daily practice, it was time to leave the center and I just wanted to stay. I just wanted to sit in that hall, wander through those gardens, and meditate for the rest of my life. But I had to get back to the band, to obligations and commitments.

For two weeks, I got up at 5:00 a.m. to meditate for an hour and then get on with my day, at the recording studio, in the plane, on stage…and at the end of every day I would sit and meditate for one hour. But peace eluded me. I felt too sensitive, too raw. I did not like the life I was living as a rock star; I just wanted to meditate. I was addicted to the feeling of it. And so, I stopped.

It took me 20 years to practice Vipassana again. I saw a little paper flyer on a Whole Foods supermarket notice board inviting practitioners of Vipassana to gather together for a full day of meditation at a town hall in Santa Monica. I was in the middle of my training for my commercial pilot certificate and stressed out with the volume of information I was trying to absorb. I took a day away from the world and at 8 a.m. on a Saturday entered the hall with about twenty other people. We all nodded to each other and lowered our eyes, entering Grand Silence. It felt amazing to sit and arrange my blanket around me as the person at the front of the hall pressed start on a smart device and I heard the mellifluous tones of S.N. Goenka again. I focused on the breath flowing out across my upper lip and then took that awareness sweeping through my body up and down as he crooned "equanimity, equanimity, equanimity." Ten hours flashed by in an instant.

The most beautiful thing about Vipassana meditation is that once you learn how to do it, all you need is yourself and your breath. The tools for this meditation are always within you.

Vipassana centers are dotted all over the world. The retreats are so popular now, you need to sign up in advance! Find out more at www.dhamma.org.

## POTENT

### YOGA

Becoming a serious yoga practitioner is a dream adventure that can take you to places of consciousness and life experience that you would never have without the discipline of the practice.

> *My body is my temple, my asanas are my prayers"*
> —B.K.S. Iyengar, founder of modern yoga

My yoga journey started in a dedicated way thirty years ago. Although in the past there have been periods of time that I did not practice regularly, I have practiced regularly for the last eleven years, to the point of becoming a teacher myself when my guru who I had been a religious student of for seven years had to leave the Caribbean island we lived on and she "gave me" her students.

In my manifesto *The Art of Witch* published in 2019 (Rockpool Publishing) there is a chapter on "Witchy Yoga" describing how Witches can benefit from the practice and how the 8-limbed path of yoga (of which the actual poses are only one path) corresponds and correlates to the gaining of powers and wisdom that a modern Witch seeks to experience throughout their journey of ritual, learning, and practice.

When I first tried yoga, decades ago, it was really hard to find a class. There was one woman offering a one-hour Saturday morning experience of Hatha yoga in a local hall. We lay on beach towels on the hard floor and had a stretch together.

Now, yoga has exploded in the West and it's fantastic! I recently joined a local studio nearby where I was based for a month to write the home stretch of this book and loved being instructed every day. It's great to be a student again.

So, explore yoga fearlessly. Just get to a class. Start somewhere and continue somewhere. Every moment on the mat adds up.

Yoga at Home on the Island...at age 53!

The effects of yoga on my life are more on the inside than on the outside, I think. The asanas, even when taught as a "workout" place you inside the temple that is your physical form and allow you to explore, understand, and clean it out! Practicing yoga cannot help but affect you spiritually in a positive way. It puts you in touch with the Spirit element of your life and helps you weave all other elements of it together, without even thinking about it. Just by doing the practice.

## TEMAZCAL RETREATS

In January of 2020, I was living in a village in Mexico called San Pancho. My yoga guru was living there with her family and I spent many happy days with them. She and I had heard about a mysterious place in the forest that was offering temazcal experiences. We both did not drink nor do drugs and wondered if this experience was one of "those ones" where people took plant medicines like ayahuasca and crammed themselves into a small space and tripped. What did we know?

Every second Saturday morning we were told that a sober temazcal retreat was offered at this location and so we decided to sign up.

When we arrived at the location the couple that owned the property welcomed us. They were so lovely and the energy of the entire place was very welcoming and grounded, and not "druggy." There were other people gathering who were super chill and friendly. My sober sensibilities were reassured.

We were led as a group to a structure that looked like a pizza oven with thick Aztec-designed mats draped over it strategically. It was explained to us that we would be entering this structure to sit for an hour and the ceremony conducted within would be of music and sound. The couple would lead, and also be in charge of pouring water on the hot rocks which were being carried into the space from a nearby fire pit by a young assistant who had a thick beard and a body covered in Aztec tattoos.

They told us that the temazcal ceremony goes beyond a physical benefit; it is a spiritual experience that helps us balance mind, body, and Spirit. There would be a few seconds "break" every 15 minutes, when the blankets would be lifted for a few moments. It was at this time we could leave if we needed to. I had decided that there was no way I was leaving, that I would sit the entire ceremony through, even though more and more people were arriving and I was truly wondering how we were all going to fit in there.

Preparation for the Temazcal

Dappled sunlight peeked through the canopy of leaves around us as we stood in the shade, but the temazcal structure was exposed to the baking hot sun. Everything was heating up, including a trickle of apprehension inside me as sweat started to gather under my arms.

We were instructed to stand in single file to enter the temazcal and as we approached the entrance, we had the option to inhale strong tobacco from a pipe offered. I declined.

I felt a tiny amount of claustrophobia hit as twenty people squeezed into the tiny space and all the blankets were closed. I was sitting cross-legged with my knees touching my guru to my left and a stranger to my right. As the last blankets closed, it was very dark and there was only a low glow from the pit with the rocks in the center of the room which was mostly obscured by the row of people in front of me. I felt my chest tighten and I struggled to take a breath…then the cacophony of drumming and singing started so loud my ears were hurting.

For a moment I felt I had to get out, I couldn't breathe…but I tried to relax and commit to my decision to stay no matter what. I observed my breath and teetered on feeling there wasn't enough oxygen to even take a breath…but then I had a powerful vision. A tree was growing in front of me—it had a huge trunk and arching expansive branches and deep roots. It was huge and casting a giant shadow and it said, "Look at me! Can you not see there is enough life in here for us all?!" I was immediately cocooned in a comforting sense of being held in a soft blanket, crouched in this upright fetal position, sweat pouring off me. I no longer thought about breathing. I was suspended in another dimension. There was enough life in there for us all.

There were breaks, and the blankets were flung open for a moment and then closed again, and we spun off back into the loud, hot darkness.

It was over quickly in a way…and as we left the temazcal, all drenched in sweat as we crawled out in single file—I looked up as I exited and stood and the man in front of me had a giant tattoo on his back…of my tree!! It was extraordinary.

I asked him about it and he said he took ayahuasca in the temazcal and he had a vision of this tree, so he got it tattooed on his back. I told him how I had seen the tree and it spoke to me and he said the tree had spoken to him too.

I have been sober for eleven years in a program now and I was nine years sober when this happened. It was very interesting to me that the tree spoke to both of us—him under the influence and me not.

I saw that shadow of the tree everywhere after that—lying on the beach I saw it in the dark patterns of branches shadowed in the sand. It was imprinted on the land and on my soul. I loved my time in San Pancho. It was where I meditated with Buddhists and took sunrise and sunset walks that were steeped in present-moment divine comprehension and bliss. Shortly after this time, COVID happened, and for the next two years the world went mad. How blessed I was to have had this time.

> **TEMAZCAL CEREMONIES**
>
> *"This is one of the oldest and most important ceremonies of the Indian Nations in America. In Mexico it was practiced since prehispanic times. Temezcal is a ceremonial and therapeutic steam bath. Participants enter inside a structure like an igloo, outside are heated volcanic stones in a ceremonial fire, which are then introduced little by little within the Temazcal. Sometimes different medicinal herbs and incense such as copal, sage, cedar, rosemary, lavender, chamomile are placed on the rocks. The benefits of the Temazcal are many, toxins are eliminated from the body through sweating, which stimulates and oxygenates the organs, strengthens the immune system, and allows for enlightened states of conscious being."—nayaritwild.com.mx*

And I have so much gratitude and respect for the couple who conducted the ceremony. Sitting over the hot fire in the center of the temazcal, facilitating ceremonies multiple times a month, they truly were warriors of freedom and enlightenment in the little clay oven in the middle of the forest.

# PASSIONATE

## MEDITATION

There are so many smartphone apps, YouTube videos, and streaming network content like that offered on the platform *Gaia* that can bring expert meditation instruction and frameworks into your living room. To explore the element of Spirit at a passionate level, I suggest committing to a practice of mediation every day.

    I really love the Calm app. I have had it on my phone now for five years. I have a very active mind, and at times have suffered from chronic insomnia. In addition to meditation guidance, the app offers bedtime stories too, which I really love! I play them every night to help me drift off to sleep. The stories create restful, positive, and expansive concepts that leave only the residue of wonder and awe as I dive into dreamland. Much better than leaving the TV on and being indoctrinated with negativity!

## ASTRONOMY

I have recently become a keen amateur astronomer. It excites me to see the sense of wonder and awe that I have been observing in meditation anchored in the physical night sky. It's fantastic to understand how astrology works when you study the constellations by actually looking at the sky and not at a chart on the table.

    Broome is a very remote town at the top end of Western Australia. About ten miles outside of town, planted firmly in the outback, is a place where you can take an "Astro Tour." You enter the property by driving down a red dirt driveway to then stop and get out to open and close behind you a large iron gate latched with a chain and a thick metal pin.

    Another 500 feet and you enter a clearing to park next to where a hundred bucket-style swivel chairs are arranged stadium style around a platform upon which thirty high-powered stargazing telescopes stand. I was so excited to be there, and when astronomer Greg Quicke walked out with his flowing white beard (earning him the nickname "Space Gandalf") me and the rest of the crowd felt like we were in the presence of a rock star. Greg is a self-taught astronomer who has a completely unique way of explaining the universe and the stars…and how, at sunset, our planet turns away from the part of the sky that the sun appears to be in. (He calls this, "Earth Turning Consciousness.") I almost felt a touch of motion sickness as his explanations made me acutely feel for a moment the speed with which the earth is rotating while at the same time revolving around the sun.

> *Giving people a living breathing conscious experience of being on a planet that is turning as it hurtles through space is our most profound task with Astro Tours.*
>
> *With this experience comes an ability to see things for what they really are, to see yourself in relation to the whole and to know that everything is on track. So relax, have fun and enjoy the ride."*
>
> —Greg Quicke: www.astrotours.net

## Elemental Science

Earth revolves around the sun at a rate of about 67,000 miles per hour (107,000 km/hr or nearly 30 km/s). At the same time, earth rotates around its axis at about 1,000 miles per hour (460 m/s or 1,600 km/hr).

## SEEING WITH SPIRIT

When I was in Mexico in January 2020, I had the opportunity to meditate regularly with a Buddhist group. We were focused on Guru Rinpoche—he is known to Buddhists as the Second Buddha, born into enlightenment; he did not have to study or be a disciple. He appeared at the center of the lotus, fully awakened—a source of primordial wisdom for the benefit of all sentient beings. He reveals the teachings of the highest nature of what it is to be.

In meditation on his image, I closed my eyes and left my body. I became aware of Guru Rinpoche next to me. We were in space…well, some kind of "space." It was completely dark but full of potential—I was aware that Guru Rinpoche had a "billowing shape" but I could not "see" as I was using my Spirit eyes. He said to me in English, "Do you want to know why humans exist?" "Yes," I replied with my mind. He said, "Open your eyes."

And I opened my human eyes…and all the galaxies, and nebulae, and billowing gas clouds appeared. We were in space, and I could see with my human eyes. And I knew that we humans exist so that we can witness creation…and it can know itself through us. In all the pain and all the loss, and all the joy and abundance, we are meant to be. We are wanted. We are all essential.

And every time I look into the night sky wherever I am on the planet, I know this.

Two hours later, I was hooked on astronomy and stargazing.

I had achieved earth-turning consciousness. I knew star names, constellations, and where to find the planets. In two short hours my life had changed forever.

Since then I have hunted out astro tours in Joshua Tree, where we wore night vision goggles to spot UFOs while being told the shamanic myths and legends of the original Cahuilla Native American peoples of the desert; the Eastern Desert of Egypt, where a Bedouin man in smock and turban held up a high-powered lazer flashlight to point out the North Star, Polaris, that his people have used for centuries to navigate across the sands at night; the Griffith Observatory in Los Angeles where seven million people have put their eye against the Zeiss 12-inch refracting lens to look at the moon since 1935; and anywhere I am at night with an app on my phone called iUniverse that I can point to the night sky and be shown exactly what I'm looking at as far as humans have determined it should be labelled.

In an age of plastic, extreme consumerism, and all the pollution that arises from modern day life, one of the most extreme and invasive forms of pollution is actually light pollution. It affects not only animal migration, insect reproduction, and sea turtle egg laying… but also our innate sense of place and purpose on the planet. Earlier humans could gaze at the night sky and see millions more stars and astronomical phenomenon…minus the distractions of misleading satellites and Starlink internet satellite constellations. (I saw these launch in a string of 13 evenly paced lights when I was in Egypt recently and was so excited to think I may be seeing UFOs and so broken-hearted when I found out they were very much identified.)

## WHERE CAN I GO WHERE THERE IS NO LIGHT POLLUTION?

The International Dark-Sky Association (IDA) is an Arizona-based nonprofit founded in 1988 with the mission "to protect and preserve the world's night skies for present and future generations."

The organization is an authority on light pollution, and through its International Dark Sky Places program, the IDA recognizes places that preserve and protect the night sky through Dark Sky Reserves and other Dark Sky Places.

## DARK SKY RESERVES

Where are the International Dark Sky Places located? As of January 2023, there are 201 certified Dark Sky Places in the world. These include 115 Parks, 38 Communities, 20 Reserves, 16 Sanctuaries, 6 Urban Night Sky Places, and 6 Dark Sky Friendly Developments of Distinction.

## THE DARKEST PLACE IN THE WORLD

Using 11 million photometers from 44 of the darkest places, a study concluded that Roque de los Muchachos Observatory, located in the Canary Islands, is the darkest place on Earth.

Here is the Top Nine List of Darkest Places recommended by the IDA where you can go to have an Astro tour…and I added number 10.

- Flagstaff Arizona,
- Galloway Forest Park, Scotland
- Chaco Canyon National Park, New Mexico
- Big Bend National Park, Texas
- Kerry International Dark Sky Reserve, Ireland
- Aoraki Mackenzie Dark Sky Reserve, New Zealand
- Namibrand Nature Reserve, Namibia
- Utah's International Dark Sky Parks
- Atacama Desert, Chili
- Broome, Western Australia and Greg Quicke's Astro Tour

## STARGAZING

Are you craving to plan the rest of your lifetime's holidays around stargazing? Here are five more of the best places to go…

### USA: MAUNA KEA OBSERVATORY

The dormant volcano of Mauna Kea on Big Island in Hawaii is a unique mountain. It's the highest point in the islands, looming a massive 13,802 feet above the Pacific Ocean. Much of it is underwater, and if measured from the sea floor to its summit, it's 33,000 ft tall, making it higher than Everest! However, its greatest gift is the view of the stars. The summit has some of the best conditions for stargazing anywhere in the world, and the Kama'āina Observatory, located right on top, exists to take advantage of this. You can't visit the observatory, but there's a point at the 9,200-meter level of the mountain where you can partake of the free stargazing program every evening from 6 p.m. to 10 p.m. You will be shown a short video on the importance of the mountain, after which high-powered telescopes are set up by the staff for you to gaze at the universe to your heart's content. There is also a star tour, where you will learn of the celestial objects that are visible that night. If the experience leaves you wanting more, head over to the 'Imiloa Astronomy Center at Hilo for its stunning planetarium and other astronomical experiences.

### USA: VERY LARGE ARRAY

Remember that shot of a vast plain glittering with white radio telescopes from the science fiction movie *Contact*? Well, it's a real-life radio observatory called the Very Large Array (VLA) located on the San Agustin Plains of New Mexico. At a height of 6,970 ft above sea level, the VLA forms a vital component of the National Radio Astronomy Observatory.

The 27 antennae monitor and investigate a vast swathe of space and astronomical objects, looking into the working of radio galaxies, quasars, supernovas, and whatever else shows up! It's a thrilling place to visit! And you can do so any day of the year. The VLA is open to visitors every day from 8:30 a.m. to sunset, and you can take a self-guided walking tour. The tour takes you to one of the working antennae and you can get a sense of the astronomical work that the radio telescope does. You can also view an award-winning film on the VLA at the visitors' center, narrated by the actress Jodie Foster. Guided tours of the facility are offered on the first Saturday of every month. These tours last for 45 minutes and culminate in a free guided viewing of the night sky through a telescope located at the campus of NM Tech in the nearby town of Socorro. The VLA is an 80 km (about 50 miles) drive from the city of Albuquerque in New Mexico.

## CHILE: THE PARANAL OBSERVATORY

Located in the trackless wastes of Chile's Atacama Desert, overlooking the Pacific Ocean in the distance, the telescopes of the Paranal Observatory are some of the most cutting-edge in the world. One of the three observing sites of the European Southern Observatory (the other two are in La Silla and Chajnantor, also in Chile), the Very Large Telescope array at Paranal is the flagship observatory. Composed of not one, but four "Unit Telescopes", it produces images four billion times sharper than what can be seen by the naked eye. The height of the site, at over 8,000 ft, also helps to make Paranal one of the finest places to observe the sky, second only to Mauna Kea. Right now, Paranal is leading the search for exoplanets in distant galaxies, and, as you can imagine, the VLA array at Paranal is on my bucket list! The observatory allows weekend visits for free guided tours of the facility. While on the tour, you will be taken to the VLA platform and enter one of the enclosures to see the main telescope. You can also visit the control room where the astronomers work, and visit the uniquely built base where all the people working at the observatory live, the Paranal Residencia.

## SOUTH AFRICA: SOUTH AFRICA ASTRONOMICAL OBSERVATORY, SUTHERLAND

If you've visited Cape Town, you might have heard the famous "noon gun" that's fired every day from Signal Hill. What you might not know is that it's fired at 12 p.m. by a time signal generated by the South African Astronomical Observatory, or SAAO, located at Sutherland in the Northern Cape. This observatory, with its many major telescopes, including the famous SALT (South African Large Telescope) probe and investigate the night sly for the secrets of the universe. The headquarters of the SAAO is situated in Cape Town, which you can visit for its planetarium and collection of historic telescopes. However, a trip some 370 km (about 230 miles) inland is a must if you wish to see the site where the actual observing takes place. The Day Tour includes a guided walk through the Visitor Center and a tour of some of the main telescopes including the SALT, the largest single optical telescope in the southern hemisphere. Night Tours include the viewing of the night sky through two specially designated visitor telescopes. However, you can't visit any of the research telescopes as astronomers would be at work.

## ENGLAND: GREENWICH OBSERVATORY

To give it its proper name, the Royal Observatory, Greenwich in London is one of the most prestigious sites associated with astronomy in the world. Home to the Prime Meridian that literally splits the world in two, as well as lending its name to the basis of determining global time zones with the Greenwich Meridian Time (it's called Universal Time, or UT, these days) the observatory has played an important role in the history of astronomy. Although all scientific work has long been shifted out to other locations, the observatory continues to function as a museum to astronomy. There's much to see and do here, but here are a couple of things you must absolutely do. The first of these is a visit to the observatory itself. Set atop a small hill overlooking the Thames, go on a day-long self-guided beginning at the Meridian Courtyard, where you can see the famous brass strip that signifies the Meridian Line. Learn about the many stories associated with the observatory (built in 1676), visit the Astronomer Royal's house, make some solar observations and participate in science demonstrations. You should also attend a Planetarium Show presented live by a Royal Observatory astronomer. It's a great way to explore the solar system as well as thrilling deep space objects.

Astro tours are extreme in their own way, even if they are not huge physical challenges. Deep space astronomy and contemplating the magnificence of the universe with what humans have developed so far to observe it is extremely awe-inspiring and will get your heart racing with excitement and your mind exploding with wonder just like if you were to jump out of an airplane in excitement!

# SOBRIETY

Is this suitable to include in an extreme adventure guide? Getting sober in a program almost 11 years ago at the time of writing has been the best adventure of my entire life. I intend it to be one that will never stop until I am no longer breathing nor feel my heart beating. It is the ultimate passion that courses through my every waking and sleeping moment and the ultimate experience of Spirit. The deepest way to connect and express it. My sobriety weaves together all the elements of my life. And I offer that maybe it could for yours too, even if you are not a recovering alcoholic like me.

As a sober human, the opportunity to explore what our bodies, these vessels of Spirit that we inhabit, are capable of is amplified.

# PERSONAL EVOLUTION

The final extreme Spirit adventure I would like to offer you to explore is your life. And how you can approach ageing as personal evolution.

I have often been told that I appear to defy the "aging process." I am 57 at the time of writing and all the photos on the cover of this book were taken in the last two years (except the Air/skydiving one which was taken ten years ago when I was 47). How do I make my passage of time on this earth a journey of not growing older, but "growing better?"

I practice yoga daily. I eat really clean and healthy (I am mostly vegetarian), and I am always exploring states of consciousness and comprehension of existence. I am creative in some way every day. I have extreme adventures as often as possible! Every day, especially the most difficult ones, is an opportunity to practice what I preach!

## ESSENTIAL OILS TO ALIGN WITH SPIRIT

Rose

Roman chamomile

Lavender

Clary sage

Frankincense

Myrrh

## SPIRIT MEDITATION BLEND

3 drops rose

2 drops frankincense

1 drop myrrh

Mix in a ¼ cup of jojoba or olive oil and massage into your feet. It may seem unusual to do this when you are seeking to open the crown chakra to connect with a sense of universal purpose, but I have found that how our feet feel as we walk in the physical world dramatically affects our innate connection to life. It may be a combination of acupressure points that are stimulated. But I also think it's something more esoteric.

I always wash my feet before bed. I never don't do this! No matter where I am in the world, no matter what extreme adventures I have or haven't had that day, no matter how "clean" my feet are. It's an energetic release. Doing this helps you process and connect with the greater intelligence behind life and inside you.

Is this the key to living a youthful dynamic life with the blessings of wisdom and evolving age? Maybe. I don't think it's just genetic because my other biological family members are not like this! Whatever it is, I would have to say that the most extreme adventure I've ever experienced or will ever experience, is my life itself. And I like this. It means I always have a reason to feel excited and motivated to keep living every day and to just be the best me that I can, through all the fuck ups and failures, and all the magnificent successes.

## ELEMENTAL INVOCATION: SELF
### Worship and Invocation of Self to Bless All Your Efforts Because When It Comes to Spirit, Your Entire Life Is Your Biggest Extreme Adventure

Spirit blesses and inspires all of the four elements because it is the moment of ascension beyond the physical place where Spirit meets you. Where you are not bound by form and instead are given an opportunity to observe it.

Before commencing with this ritual, take a few moments to just stare at the palms of your hands—just be—sense the stardust in the core of your being…and see if you can see it "sparkle" there.

> *It is totally 100% true: nearly all the elements in the human body were made in a star and many have come through several supernovas. A new survey of 150,000 stars shows just how true this is: humans and their galaxy have about 97 percent of the same kind of atoms."*
>
> —Dr. Ashley King, Planetary scientist and stardust expert

The piece of wisdom called *Desiderata* was hung in my parents' home in a large frame and was one of the very first things I learned to read and comprehend. I started reading it when I was four…and

I understood it by the time I was seven.

It has always served as a touchstone to spirit for me. Its concepts underline my Witchcraft, my yoga, my life. And while the wording is a little older and based on some earlier Western concepts of human life, ultimately with a little self-interpretation it is timeless and transparent. Potent and powerful and intensely reassuring. It can act like the glue that holds everything together—just like Spirit weaves its way through all things. I think because it made such an impact on my very young human mind, I found it a "language" that was the first I understood. The lines, "You are a child of the Universe, no less than the trees and the stars, you have a right to be here," have always guided me back into the light from dark places.

I suggest performing this ritual on a full moon. Burn incense of frankincense and myrrh and read the *Desiderata* by the light of seven white candles.

After which, go outside and moon-gaze and contemplate that the Universe is yours and you are blessed. Standing in the moonlight, say the most powerful statement of worship to any God or Goddess.

Invoke yourself…your direct connection to the divine in your name and on your terms:

*I honor thee (your name)*
*I honor your divine presence*
*I honor your magnificence*
*I honor thee (your name)*

---

### DESIDERATA

*Go placidly amid the noise and the haste, and remember what peace there may be in silence. As far as possible, without surrender, be on good terms with all persons.*

*Speak your truth quietly and clearly; and listen to others, even to the dull and the ignorant; they too have their story.*

*Avoid loud and aggressive persons; they are vexatious to the spirit. If you compare yourself with others, you may become vain or bitter, for always there will be greater and lesser persons than yourself.*

*Enjoy your achievements as well as your plans. Keep interested in your own career, however humble; it is a real possession in the changing fortunes of time.*

*Exercise caution in your business affairs, for the world is full of trickery. But let this not blind you to what virtue there is; many persons strive for high ideals, and everywhere life is full of heroism.*

*Be yourself. Especially do not feign affection. Neither be cynical about love; for in the face of all aridity and disenchantment, it is as perennial as the grass.*

*Take kindly the counsel of the years, gracefully surrendering the things of youth.*

*Nurture strength of spirit to shield you in sudden misfortune. But do not distress yourself with dark imaginings. Many fears are born of fatigue and loneliness.*

*Beyond a wholesome discipline, be gentle with yourself. You are a child of the universe no less than the trees and the stars; you have a right to be here.*

*And whether or not it is clear to you, no doubt the universe is unfolding as it should. Therefore be at peace with God, whatever you conceive Him to be. And whatever your labors and aspirations, in the noisy confusion of life, keep peace in your soul. With all its sham, drudgery and broken dreams, it is still a beautiful world. Be cheerful. Strive to be happy.*

# AFTERWORD

After many years of venerating the divine feminine, and experiencing profound connections and revelations, it only becomes even more extraordinary and breathtaking when an ancient Goddess communicates with you for the first time in a visceral and powerful way.

Fiona Offers the Final Print of this Book to Sekhmet at Karnak Temple, Luxor

Thank you Sekhmet for speaking to me in the Temple of Philae, and helping me to understand the nature of what the Gods and Goddesses want from us—which is veneration and worship, not demands and cajoling.

Worship and recognition offered sincerely and regularly opens a path for the Gods to shine their light upon us and guide our way to what is best for us.

The Gods know themselves through our recognition of them and we see ourselves reflected in them. We are their witnesses. And they know us better than we know ourselves.

I wrote this book "bookended" by two experiences in Egypt. A country in which the locals feel moved to say, "We don't live in Egypt. Egypt lives in us."

One of the oldest countries in the human world. And one in which I have felt profoundly at home.

I dedicate this book to Egypt, to Sekhmet, and to you. I hope you are inspired to live an adventurous, elemental life of divine magnificence, cultivating awe and wonder in your existence and offering this to the Divine.

Blessed Be,
Fiona Horne

# ABOUT THE AUTHOR

Fiona Horne was 19 when, in 1985, she formed Australia's first all-girl punk group, The Mothers, who recorded a vinyl 7 inch single "Drives Me Wild" and 12-inch ep called "12 Incher" on the Waterfront Label.

At the time there were few women playing guitar and singing on Australian stages and young Fiona made her mark with her fearless stage persona, defiant lyrics, and powerful guitar playing.

In 1991 she co-formed electro/rock outfit Def FX who went on to have major local and international success, topping the independent charts consecutively, receiving an ARIA nomination for Best Independent Album in 1993, plus regular appearances in JJJ's Hottest 100—Australia's leading radio network.

Major label signings to EMI, RCA/BMG and Universal lead to

mainstream chart success for Def FX.

One of Australia's hardest working live bands, in the band's seven-year career, they headlined to thousands and toured with international acts like the Smashing Pumpkins and No Doubt and performed every Big Day Out (Australia's Lollapalooza) including opening the international main stage.

The band had significant success in the USA, signed to RCA/BMG in New York, two national tours, Top 20 Billboard chart positions and high rotation on MTV. Def FX also charted in Asia in 1996, touring Japan with No Doubt.

Fiona demonstrated unique songwriting abilities in Def FX, and her strong, wild stage performances captivated audiences in Australia, Asia, and the USA.

She inspired a generation of young women in the 90's to be creative, confident, to rock hard and believe in themselves.

After Def FX, Fiona worked successfully in television and radio, hosting her own shows and with regular guest appearances on the networks Nine, Ten, Seven, and ABC, plus hosting Radio MMM's "Homegrown" and "Planet Rock" countdown. She also released a single with ABC's Paul McDermott, the ARIA charting, "Shut Up and Kiss Me," and two solo music projects.

Coinciding with her work in television, Fiona commenced a writing career as the author of sixteen bestselling books on modern Witchcraft and two oracle decks, first published in 1997 ongoing. She is now one of the world's most respected Witches, her work having a generational impact on the evolution of the Modern Witch. Her tireless devotion to dispelling negative myths and stereotypes contributes to the freedom of Modern Witches to practice their Craft today without fearing vilification and persecution.

In 2000, Fiona moved to the USA and continued working in television and radio, scoring a starring role in the Syfy Channel TV hit series, Mad Mad House, which saw her face on billboards in

Times Square and an audience of 1.6 million tuning in every week.

After a successful 10 years in Hollywood, in 2011 Fiona changed her life's direction and became a commercial pilot flying humanitarian aid in the Caribbean, which included two missions to Haiti in the wake of 2016's Hurricane Matthew that she coordinated, raised funds for and flew herself, partnering with the Good Samaritan Foundation of Haiti, plus working as captain for a private on-demand air charter company. She was the most requested captain when the lockdowns of 2020 saw the aviation industry grounded.

With so much uncertainty in the world, she returned to Australia, basing herself in Western Australia.

In 2021, Fiona returned to the Australian stage, songwriting, playing guitar, and singing in two projects: an acoustic duo Spiff & Fifi (which hit Number 1 in the Australian Country Radio Charts in July that year) and original rock band, SEAWITCH (whose debut album entered the independent charts at Number 2 in November 2022).

Once again, Fiona was inspiring women of all ages and backgrounds to be confident and free to express themselves musically.

In addition to mentoring young female musicians, Fiona volunteered at her local community radio station, Radio Margaret River, producing and hosting "Sistars." Every fortnight she interviewed local female artists and showcased their music and art.

Throughout flying and playing music again, Fiona returned to the laptop, when in 2017 Australian publisher, Rockpool Publishing/Simon & Schuster, invited her to write again, leading to three internationally published books and bestsellers in their genre: 2017's autobiography, The Naked Witch, 2019's manifesto, The Art of Witch, and 2021's Teen Magick-Witchcraft for a New Generation. Fiona also released a debut Oracle deck, The Magick of You, to acclaim in 2019.

In August 2023, Dark Magick Oracle—Reveal the Light Within (Rockpool Publishing) continued Fiona's shining presence in the oracle world.

She has another upcoming oracle deck, The Lost Oracle, due for release in 2024, and more publishing projects on the horizon.

In 2023 she announced her spiritual adventure experiences for women, leading with "Meet Yourself in Egypt" to a very positive response—her first trip selling out in just 72 hours. She will be offering regular: "Meet Yourself in…" experiences in amazing locations around the world. Keep an eye on www.fionahorne.com to stay updated.

She plans to offer experiences for the LGBTQIA community also.

Fiona's personal passions include being a 100 ft+ freediver, world record-holding skydiver, professional firedancer, and world traveler.

**Website:** www.fionahorne.com
**Instagram:** @captainfifi
**Facebook:** @fionahorneofficial

Join Fiona's Patreon community to get to know Fiona personally—she looks forward to getting to know you! You will find Self Care Sunday motivational messages and card reading for the week, Monthly Spells, book readings (Fiona reads her books on video for you—starting with her autobiography The Naked Witch (Rockpool Publishing), which are candid, revealing, entertaining and spellbinding.

Fiona's books take on a whole new energy when Fiona reads them herself and offers extra behind the scenes anecdotes and insights. And there is more at her Patreon: monthly Q&A get togethers, one-on-one time for personal readings, and life coaching. And even lots more! Take a look and experience the magick and adventure Fiona offers her community as her journey continues. She would love you to come along!

www.patreon.com/fionahorne

## OTHER RECENT OFFERINGS BY FIONA

*Witch—A Magickal Journey* (20th Anniversary Edition) Harper Collins, 2018

*The Naked Witch*, Rockpool Publishing, 2017

*The Art of Witch*, Rockpool Publishing, 2019

*Magick of You Oracle*, Rockpool Publishing, 2019

*Teen Magick*, Rockpool Publishing, 2021

*Dark Magick Oracle*, Rockpool Publishing, 2023

To explore Fiona's earlier titles visit:

www.fionahorne.com/books

# Warlock Press™
WarlockPress.com

Warlock Press is an independent occult publisher that is driven to provide unequalled content written by a diverse roster of today's magical adepts. Our authors hail from a spectrum of magical traditions, but share crucial things in common: authentic practice, established credentials, thorough research, and genuine devotion. This means that you can trust that you are getting the very capstone of the pyramid of occult wisdom.

### INITIATION INTO WITCHCRAFT
### Brian Cain
*Foreword by Maxine Sanders*

This is a book about the religion of Witchcraft. It honors the old Gods, the ancient mysteries, and the secrets of magic. It is an exploration of the timeless traditions, essential ethics, and the awe-inspiring power of our Craft and provides basic practices that will help the reader to embrace the deeper ways of the Witch. It is a signpost for those seeking the path that begins the journey of initiation into Witchcraft and primer of occult techniques and rituals to prepare for that journey.

### THE WITCHES' BOOK OF THE DEAD
### Christian Day
*Foreword by Laurie Cabot*

The revised and expanded tenth-anniversary edition of this genre changing classic is available August, 2021. Readers will learn to summon and honor the spirits of the dead to bring blessings in their everyday lives, discover Witches of legend who raised the dead, and explore methods of spirit contact, necromancy, potent rituals, recipes, and exercises, and features two new chapters, new foreword, and a new preface!

## MOTHER: ECSTASY, TRANSFORMATION, AND THE GREAT GODDESS
Levi Rowland
*Foreword by H. Byron Ballard*

The Great Goddess is reclaiming her place as the preeminent force of life and creation. Devotion to Mother is a transformative experience. No matter what incarnation we invoke, she comes. She breathes into life, echoing the prayers and incantations of every initiator, Witch, believer, and devotee that has ever stood at her shrine and felt her presence, as real as anything under the sun (or beyond it). In her worship, in her magic, in her dance, is a living spiritual tradition, drawing from many sources but still focused on one multifaceted absolute. This book is a guide to the seeker who wishes to live a life turned towards the altar of the Great Goddess. Drawing from history but firmly rooted in the modern search for God the Mother, readers will be taken on an exploration of Goddess religion as a lived experience, an endless source of transformation and growth.

## MAGICK WITHOUT TOOLS
Sean Wilde
*Foreword by Lilith Dorsey*

This book is designed for everyone from absolute beginners to experienced practitioners, giving a solid foundation of background and practices for the former and new ways of looking at magic for the latter. Through the practices and rituals in this book, you will be able to start your path using magic or develop it further, possibly transforming it entirely. This book is intended for everyone. It doesn't matter your background, where your family comes from, where you live, or any other type of status. What I teach and share with you is accessible to all and is your birthright.

## VOODOO AND AFRICAN TRADITIONAL RELIGION
Lilith Dorsey

Journey beyond the basic tenets of the faiths of the African diaspora to the vibrant, living spirit world of their peoples. This seminal guide to African spirituality has been revised and expanded to include tools for activists to empower their work for social change with the wisdom of their ancestors, as well as never-before-published recipes, personal spells and charms, such as root magick for protection and protest, and devotional rituals readers can perform themselves.

## THE ART COSMIC: THE MAGIC OF TRADITIONAL ASTROLOGY
Levi Rowland
*Foreword by Sorita d'Este*

A detailed guide to the fundamentals of planetary magic using the seven sacred spheres of the ancients, including a system of celestial correspondences to use as a basis for meaningful spells, rituals, and workings. Readers will learn how to interpret natal charts using timeless methods of traditional astrology, use horary astrology for divination, incorporate the planetary hours for more successful spell work, and perform potent magical rites for each planet.

www.ingramcontent.com/pod-product-compliance
Lightning Source LLC
Chambersburg PA
CBHW072157070526
44585CB00015B/1176